Cross Stitch
Alphabets

David & Charles

A DAVID & CHARLES BOOK

First published in the UK in 2003

Designs Copyright: Sue Cook © pages 16, 32, 56, 95; Claire Crompton © pages 23, 39, 40, 48, 60,
96, 99, 103; Maria Diaz © pages 19, 43, 68, 72, 79, 80, 83, 92; Lucie Heaton © pages 8, 36, 63;
Caroline Palmer © pages 28, 31, 44, 55, 76, 84, 91; Susan Penny © pages 11, 24, 47, 51, 71, 100;
Helen Philipps © pages 35, 52, 87; Lesley Teare © pages 15, 20, 67, 88;
Anne Wilson © pages 12, 27, 84.

Photography, text and layout Copyright © David & Charles 2003

Distributed in North America
by F&W Publications, Inc.
4700 East Galbraith Road
Cincinnati, OH 45236
1-800-289-0963

A catalogue record for this book is available from the British Library.

ISBN 07153 1287 1

Designed and produced by Penny & Penny
Printed in Italy by G. Canale & C. Turin
for David & Charles
Brunel House   Newton Abbot   Devon

Contents

Introduction 7

Introduction

Alphabets have been cross stitched onto samplers since the beginning of the eighteenth century; more recently individual letters taken from alphabets have been used to create personal gifts. You will find that the wonderful alphabets in this book, some traditional, some modern, will have a great number of uses when stitched into keepsakes for family and friends. So if you are looking for a nursery gift for a new baby; wedding favours for the bride and groom; or birthday cards for people who keep pets, love gardening, or enjoy quilting, then look no further. With 50 alphabets to choose from and project ideas from monogrammed towels to ballet bags, you are sure to find just the right project waiting to be stitched.

A selection of alphabet designs clockwise from top left:
Seaside page 16; Cats page 28; Cottages page 56;
Country Farmyard page 8; Delft page 36; Summer
Garden page 32; Folk Art page 72; Noah's Ark page 80;
Celtic page 44; Nursery Rhymes page 96; Ballet page 20;
Quilters page 92; Folk Art page 72; Herbs and Flowers
page 64; Egyptian page 76; Art Nouveau page 12.

Country Farmyard

*Enjoy the rural charm and simplicity of a country farmyard
with this stunning gingham alphabet*

The jam pot cover and card were stitched on to 28 count cream evenweave fabric using DMC stranded cotton (floss), working each stitch on the chart over two threads of fabric. To make the jam pot cover, cut a circle from the stitched fabric large enough to fit over the jam pot. Neaten the edge with blanket stitch using six strands of red stranded cotton (floss). To make a matching breakfast set, stitch individual letters on to cream linen napkins.

Designed by Lucie Heaton

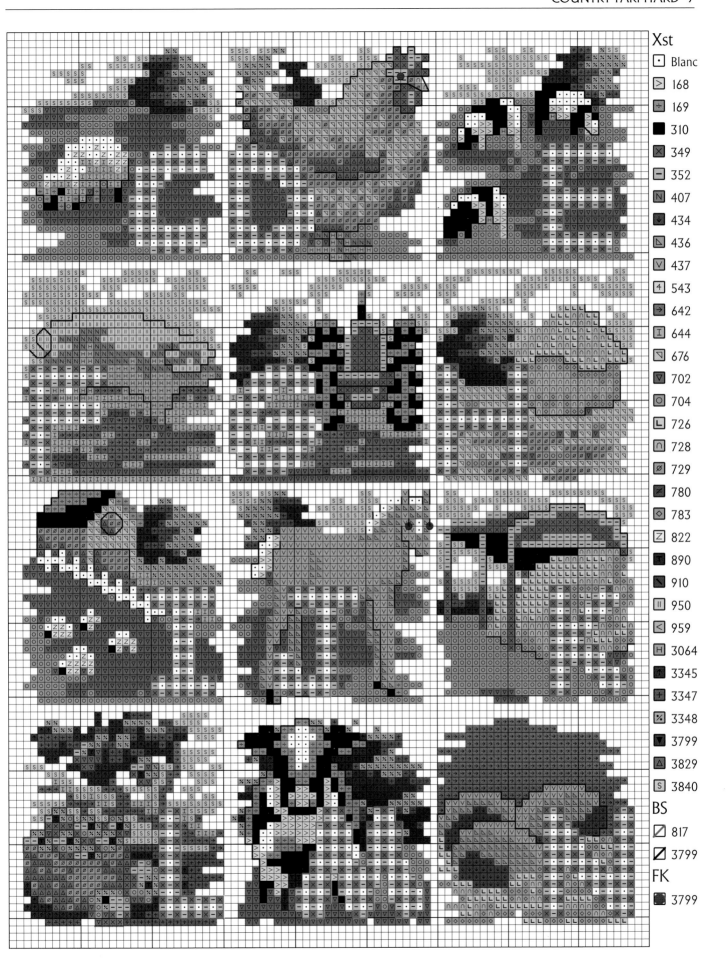

Xst

⊡	Blanc
▷	168
⊞	169
■	310
⊠	349
⊟	352
⋈	407
⬇	434
◩	436
▽	437
4	543
→	642
▯	644
◺	676
▼	702
◎	704
⌐	726
∩	728
⌀	729
⬚	780
◇	783
◪	822
■	890
◣	910
‖	950
◁	959
⊞	3064
■	3345
⊞	3347
⊠	3348
▼	3799
△	3829
ⓢ	3840

BS

⟋	817
⟋	3799

FK

⬣	3799

Xst

·	Blanc
⊳	168
+	169
■	310
⊠	349
−	352
Ν	407
↓	434
◣	436
∨	437
4	543
→	642
I	644
◹	676
▽	702
○	704
∟	726
∩	728
∅	729
▦	780
◇	783
Ζ	822
■	890
◩	910
‖	950
<	959
Η	3064
■	3345
+	3347
%	3348
◼	3799
△	3829
S	3840

BS

◿	817
◿	3799

FK

◼	3799

Sunflowers

Fresh vibrant yellows and pinks have been used to design this bright cheerful summer alphabet

Designed by Susan Penny

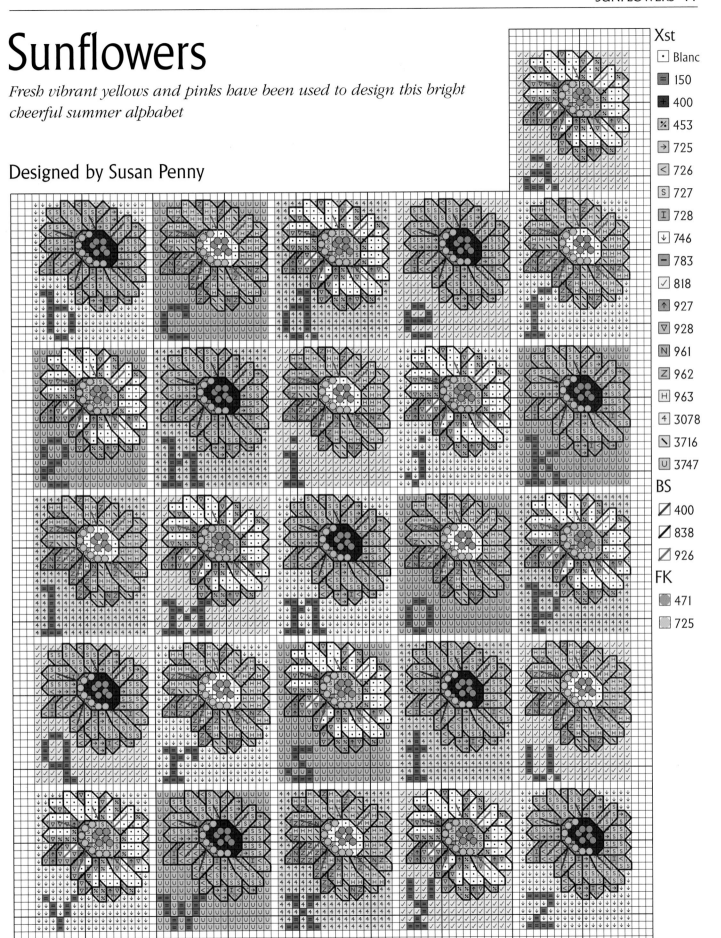

Xst
· Blanc
▬ 150
✚ 400
⊠ 453
→ 725
< 726
S 727
I 728
↓ 746
▬ 783
✓ 818
↑ 927
▽ 928
N 961
Z 962
H 963
4 3078
◹ 3716
U 3747

BS
◿ 400
◿ 838
◿ 926

FK
■ 471
□ 725

Art Nouveau

*This beautiful stylized alphabet has been inspired by the grace
and charm of the 1900s*

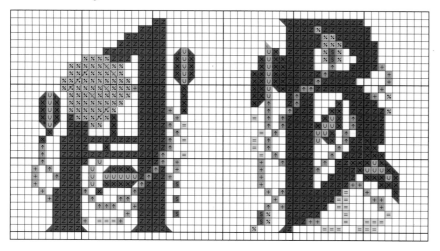

The letter on the pill pot is stitched on to 28 count white evenweave fabric, working each stitch over a single thread of fabric. Waste canvas was used to stitch the letter K on to a ready-made silk scarf. Both designs were stitched using DMC stranded cotton (floss) in the colours listed in the key.

Letters from this alphabet could be used to personalize an evening purse, make-up bag or to monogram a handkerchief.

Designed by Anne Wilson

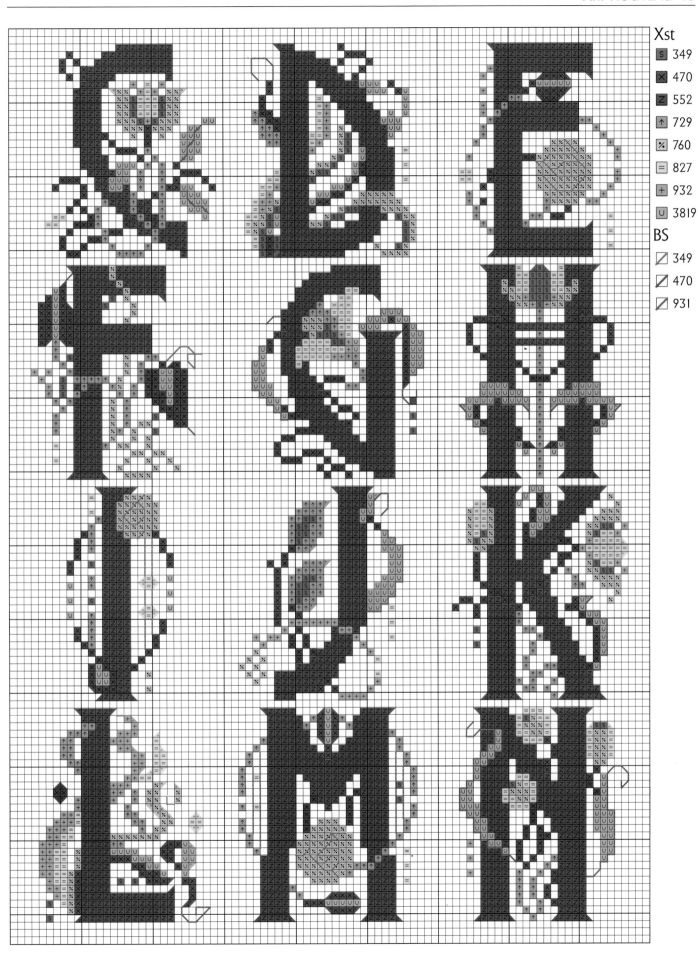

Xst
S	349
✗	470
Z	552
↑	729
⅍	760
=	827
+	932
U	3819

BS
◿	349
◿	470
◿	931

Xst

S	349
✕	470
◪	552
↑	729
⅍	760
=	827
+	932
U	3819

BS

⧄	349
⧄	470
⧄	931

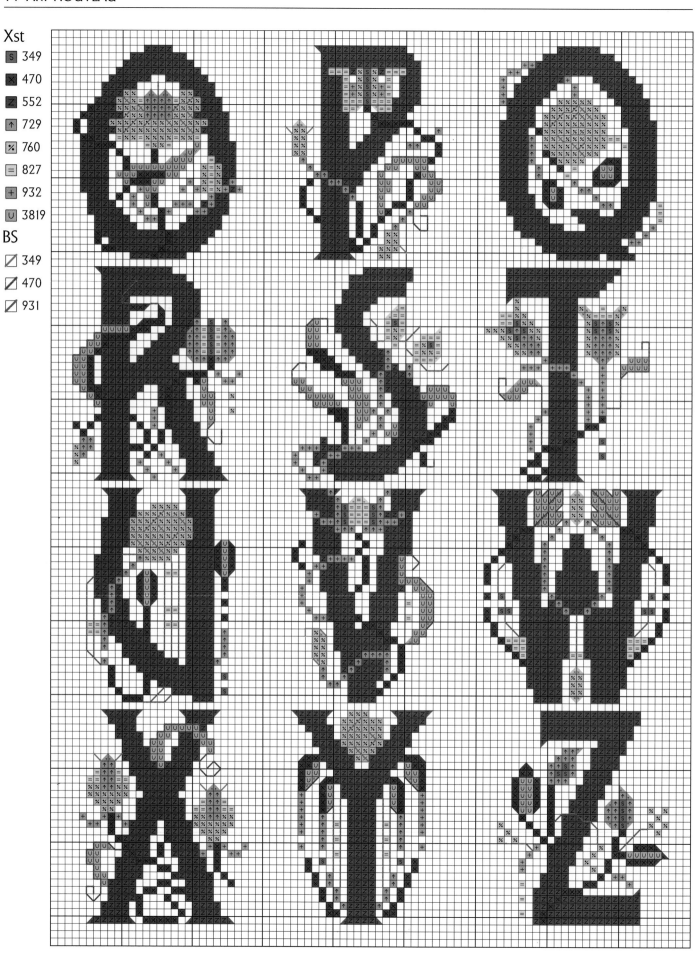

Art Deco

Bold colours and clean lines have been used to create this alphabet in the Art Deco style of the 1930s

Designed by Lesley Teare

Xst	
■	310
S	721
−	725
✳	792
V	817
⊞	3812

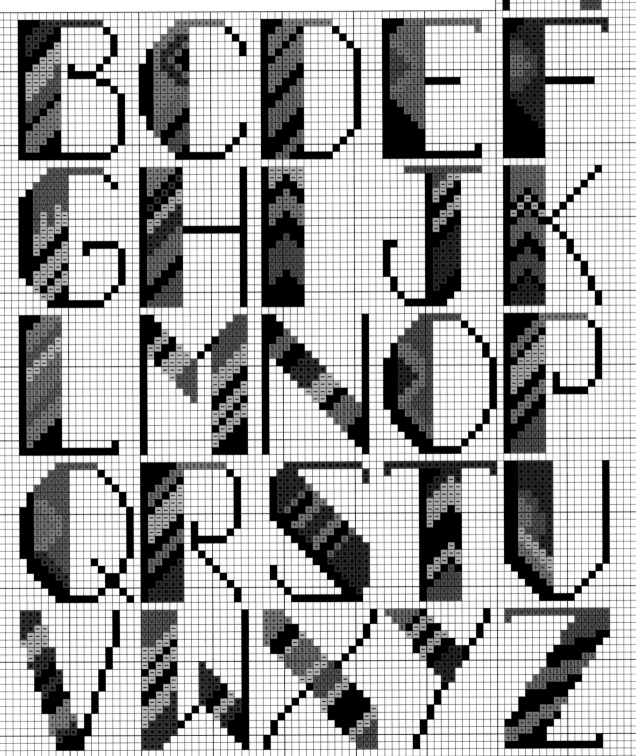

Seaside

This seaside inspired alphabet is sure to bring a smile to your face as you enjoy the colours and images of summer

The letters on the sunglass case and drinks coaster were stitched on yellow 14 count aida fabric using DMC stranded cotton (floss), as listed in the key. The sunglass case was made from padded fabric, on to which was sewn a flap cut from the stitched fabric. The curved edge of the flap was neatened with binding tape, before the flap was attached to the top of the case. The letter P was mounted in a clear acetate drinks coaster.

Designed by Sue Cook

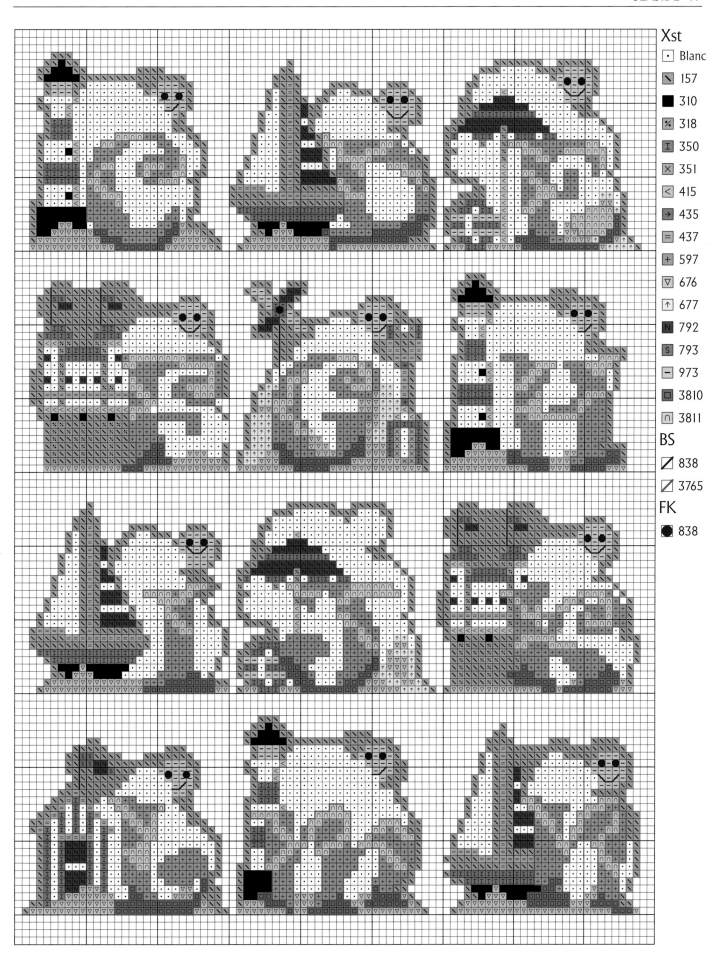

Xst
- · Blanc
- ◣ 157
- ■ 310
- ▨ 318
- ▥ 350
- ☒ 351
- ◀ 415
- ➡ 435
- ▤ 437
- ✛ 597
- ▽ 676
- ↑ 677
- ◼ 792
- ▦ 793
- ▬ 973
- ▢ 3810
- ∩ 3811

BS
- ╱ 838
- ╱ 3765

FK
- ● 838

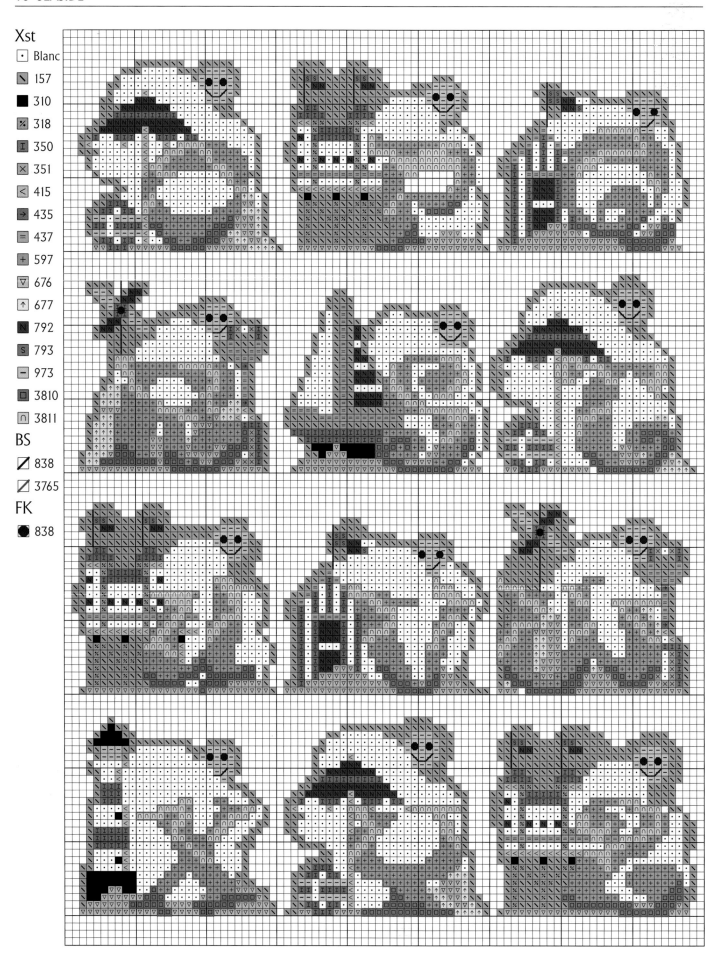

Undersea

Shells, fish and seaweed in shades of aqua and green have been used to create this delightful alphabet inspired by life beneath the waves

Designed by Maria Diaz

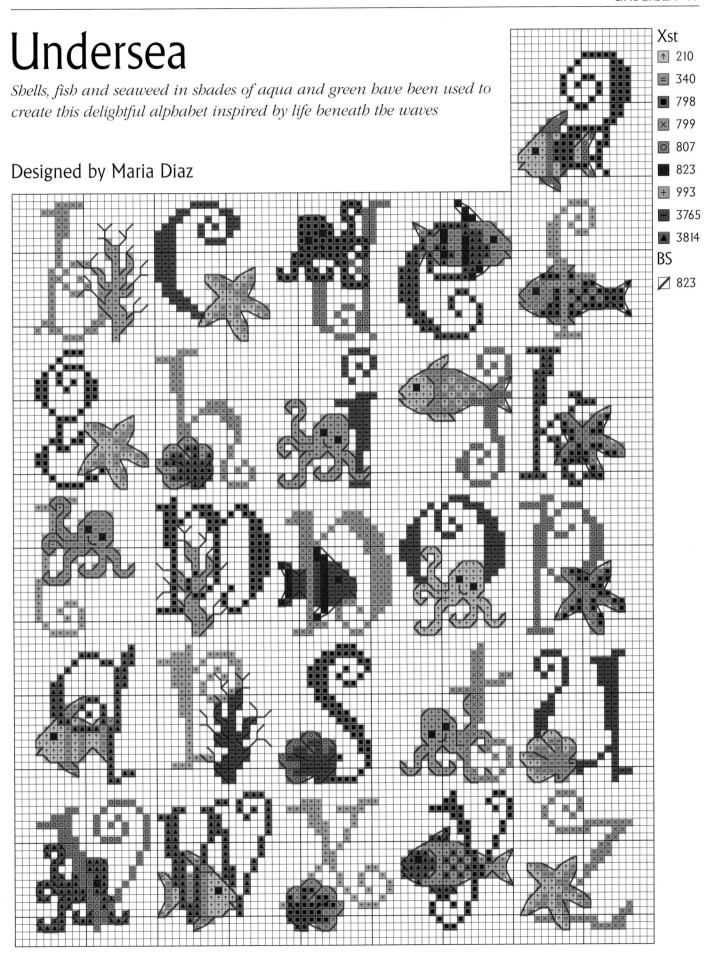

Xst	
↑	210
=	340
■	798
✕	799
◎	807
▪	823
+	993
▬	3765
▲	3814
BS	
╱	823

Ballet

This alphabet in soft pastels shows cute ballet dancers learning their steps before taking to the stage

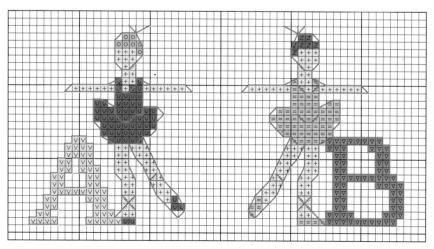

Three letters have been stitched together to personalize this pretty gingham ballet bag. The letters were worked on to 28 count antique white evenweave fabric, using DMC stranded cotton (floss), in the colours listed in the key. Each stitch on the chart was worked over two threads of fabric.

The letters from this alphabet could be used to personalize a birthday card for a very special little girl.

Designed by Lesley Teare

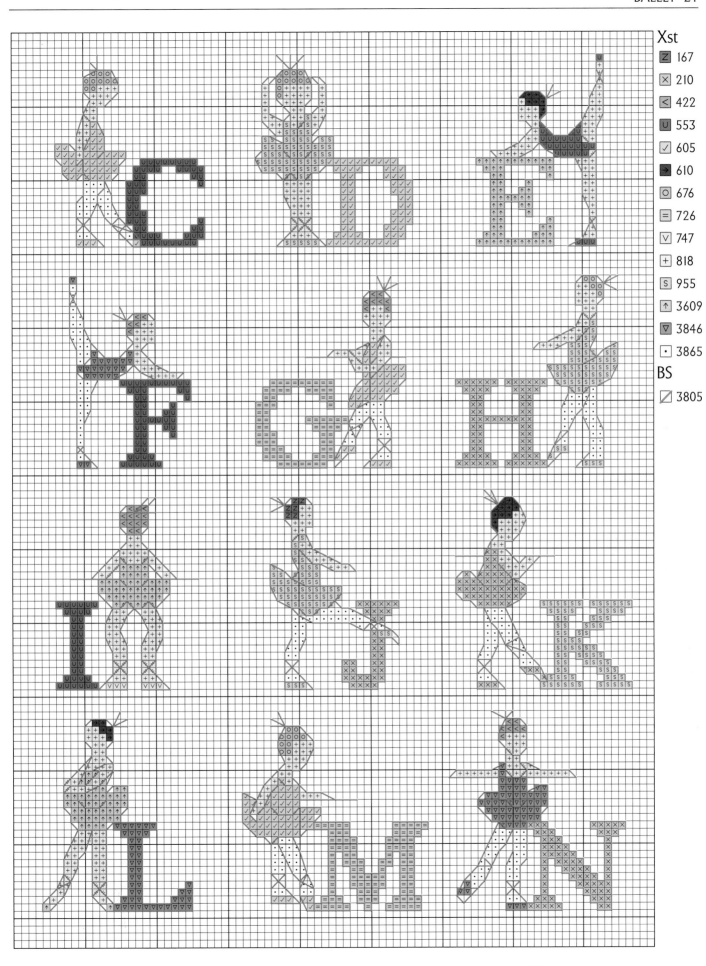

Xst

Z	167
X	210
<	422
U	553
✓	605
→	610
O	676
=	726
V	747
+	818
S	955
↑	3609
▽	3846
·	3865

BS

╱	3805

Xst

Z	167
X	210
<	422
U	553
✓	605
→	610
O	676
=	726
V	747
+	818
S	955
↑	3609
▽	3846
·	3865

BS

╱	3805

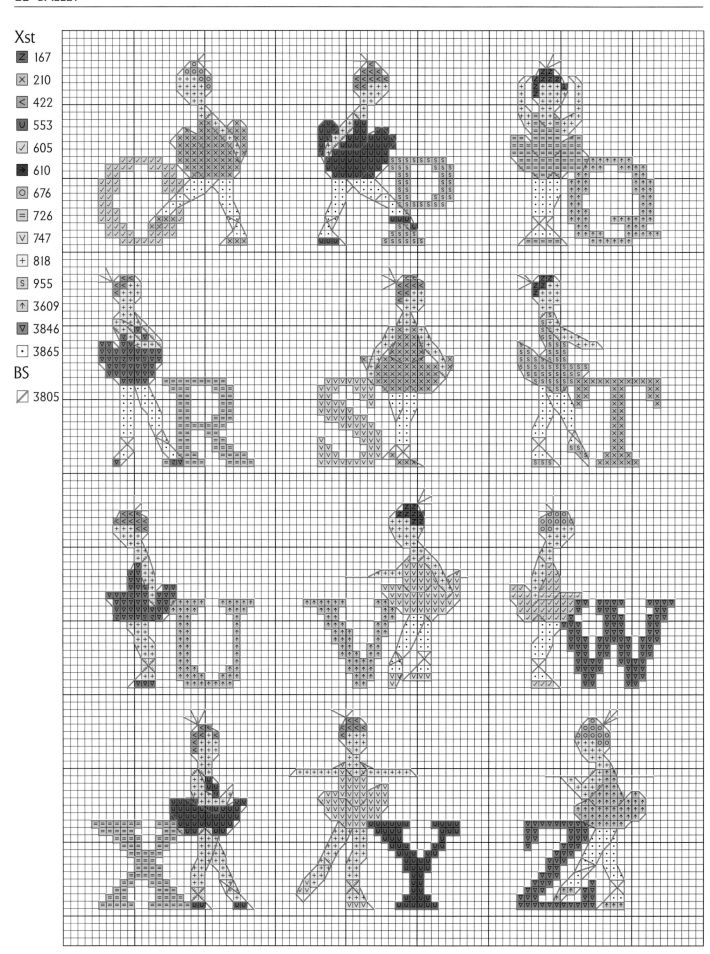

Dolls

Dolls dressed in gingham, spots, stripes and hearts; each of the cute doll letters would make a charming birthday card

Designed by Claire Crompton

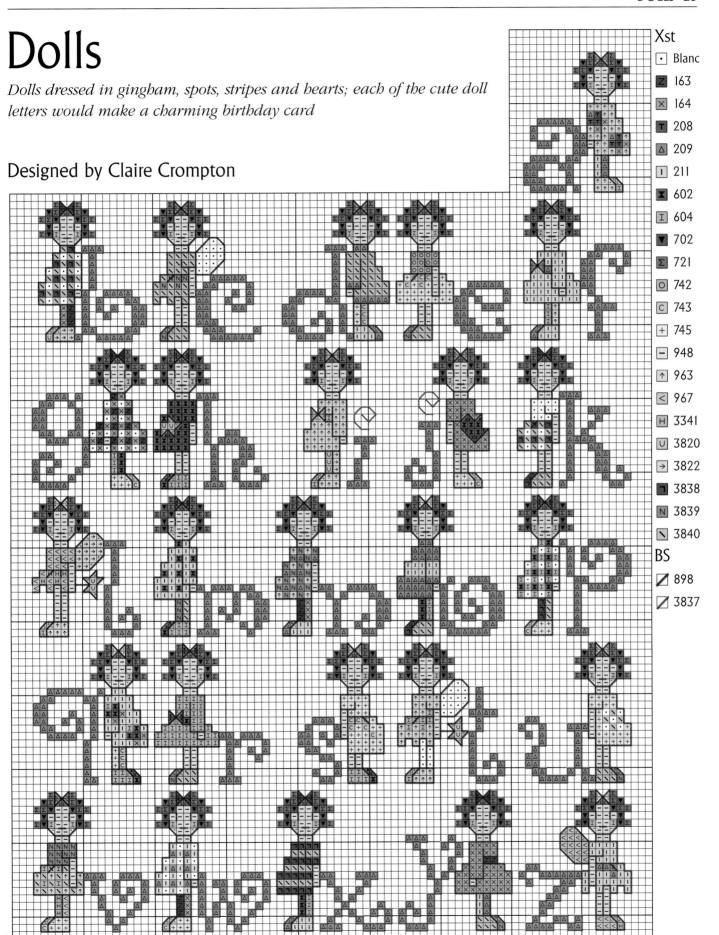

Xst	
·	Blanc
Z	163
X	164
T	208
△	209
I	211
⊠	602
I	604
▼	702
Σ	721
O	742
C	743
+	745
−	948
↑	963
<	967
H	3341
U	3820
→	3822
⌐	3838
N	3839
＼	3840

BS

⁄	898
⁄	3837

Elizabethan

*Inspired by paintings and embroideries of the Elizabethan
period, this alphabet is reminiscent of antique blackwork*

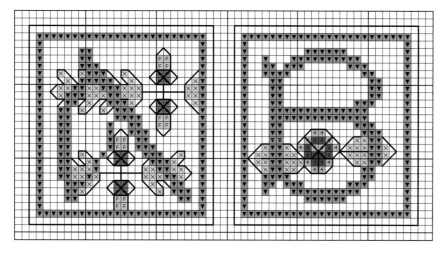

The bookmark and gift bag were stitched on
28 count cream evenweave fabric using DMC
stranded cotton (floss), working each stitch
on the chart over two threads of fabric. To
make the gift bag, sew two rectangles of
fabric together, turning over the top edge to
neaten. For the bookmark, after stitching the
letters cut two rectangles from the fabric, with
a point at one end. Stitch round the outer
edge leaving a small gap for turning. Turn
through the gap, then sew up and decorate.

Designed by Susan Penny

Xst
▯	151
▮	155
⚄	164
4	210
✕	369
←	407
S	422
→	727
=	739
▼	932
F	3047
∩	3325
−	3753
⟍	3779
U	3822
↑	3841

BS
| ╱ | 310 |

Xst

I	151
II	155
%	164
4	210
X	369
←	407
S	422
→	727
=	739
▼	932
F	3047
∩	3325
−	3753
\	3779
U	3822
↑	3841

BS

/	310

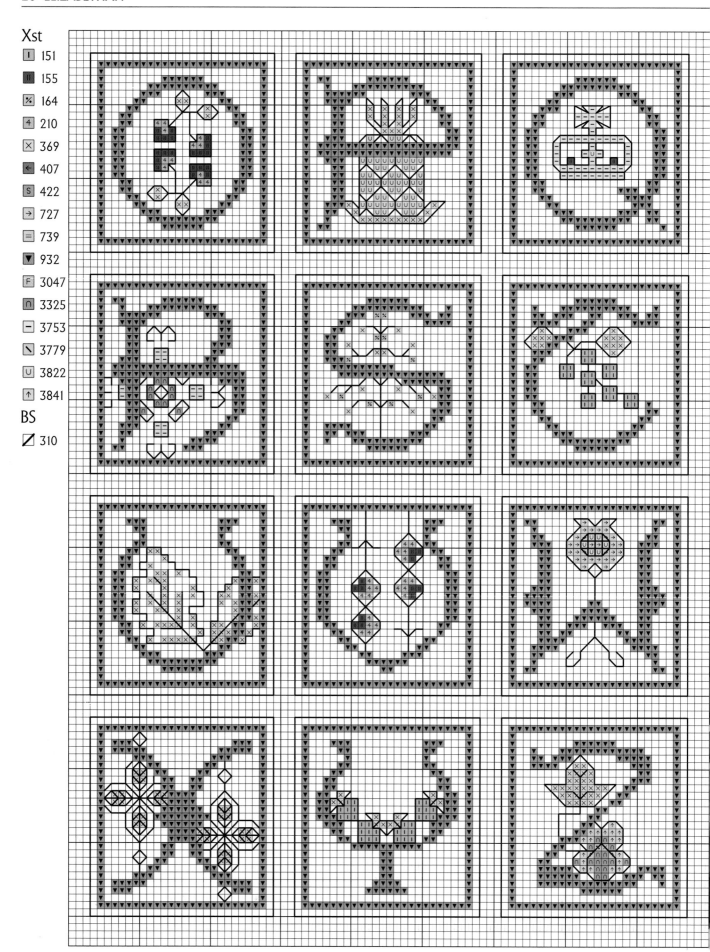

Victorian

Original Victorian lettering has been used as inspiration for this alphabet which could be used on cards or samplers

Designed by Anne Wilson

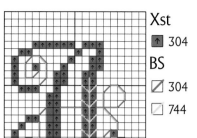

Xst	
▲	304
BS	
◸	304
◸	744

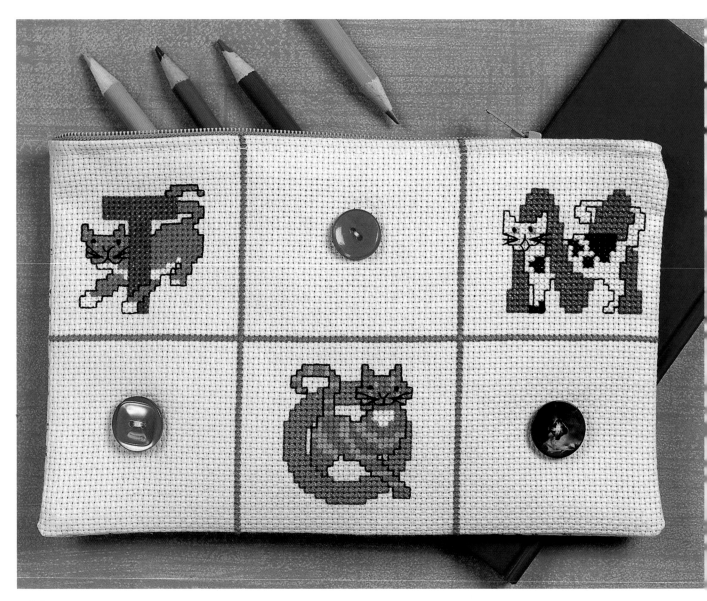

Cats

Stitched into a patchwork design these friendly felines are great fun and sure to please any cat lover

Three letters have been stitched on to pale blue 14 count aida fabric, using DMC stranded cotton (floss), as listed in the key. The letters should be separated by vertical and horizontal rows of cross stitch.

To make the pencil case, cut a rectangle of patterned fabric the same size as the stitched bag front. Sew around three sides leaving an opening at the top for the zip. Once the zip is inserted, sew buttons into the empty squares on the bag front.

Designed by Caroline Palmer

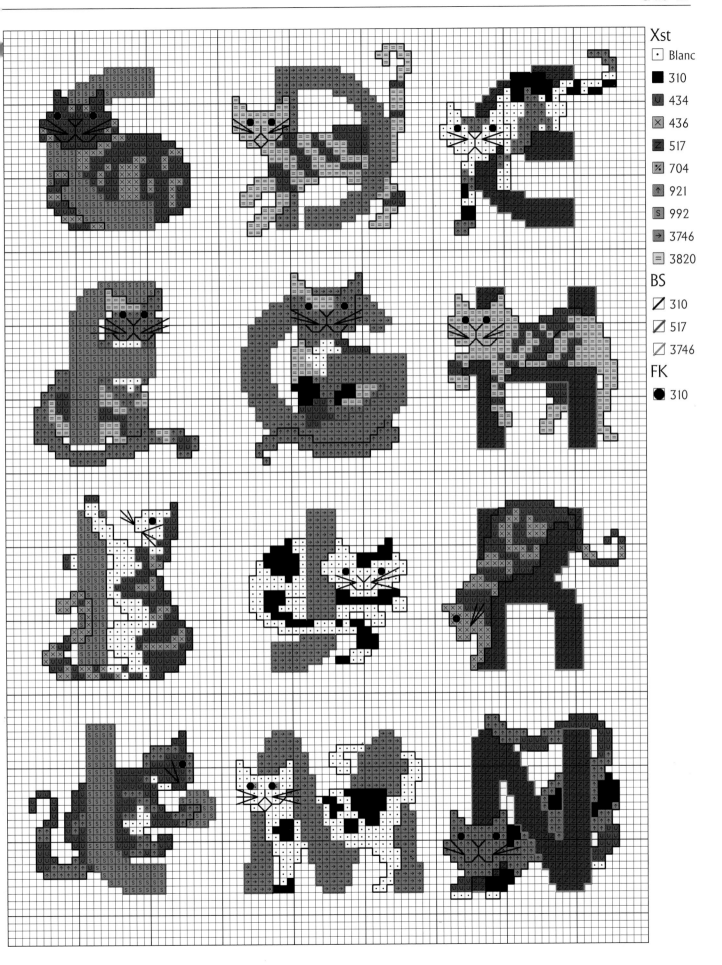

Xst
· Blanc
■ 310
U 434
× 436
▨ 517
⊠ 704
↑ 921
S 992
→ 3746
= 3820

BS
╱ 310
╱ 517
╱ 3746

FK
● 310

Xst
- · Blanc
- ■ 310
- ▨ 434
- ☒ 436
- ◪ 517
- ▨ 704
- ↑ 921
- S 992
- → 3746
- = 3820

BS
- ╱ 310
- ╱ 517
- ╱ 3746

FK
- ● 310

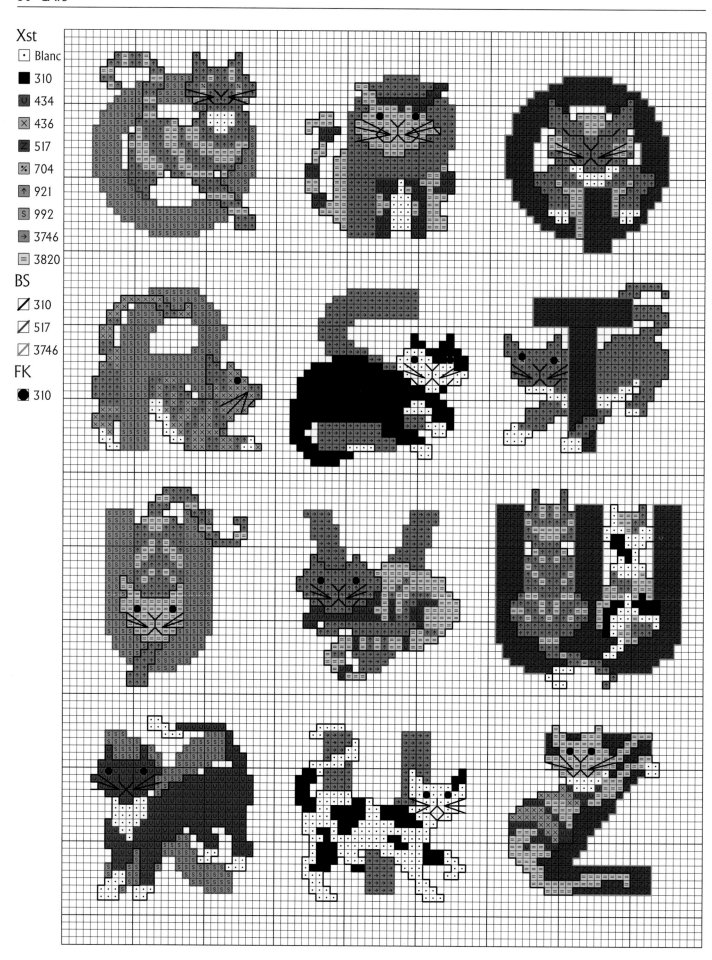

Pets

Whether you like cats, dogs, mice, fish or rabbits you are sure to love the animals in this cute and cuddly alphabet

Designed by Caroline Palmer

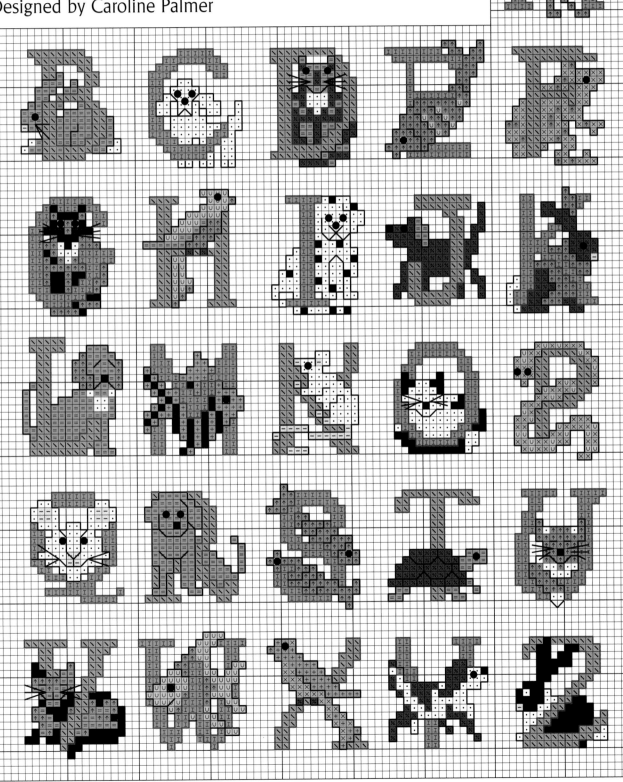

Xst	
·	Blanc
I	209
■	310
✕	368
✖	434
═	436
U	726
↑	922
─	3713
+	3755
◣	3806

BS	
╱	310
╱	915

FK	
●	310

Summer Garden

This delightful alphabet of rambling roses and butterflies is perfect for creating cards and keepsakes

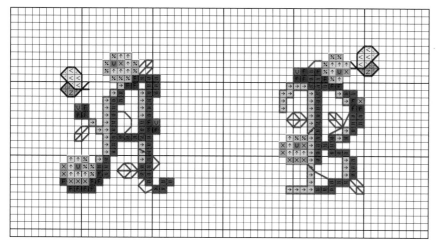

The gift bags were worked on pale blue 28 count aida fabric using DMC stranded cotton (floss), as listed in the key. Each stitch on the chart was worked over two threads of fabric. To make a bag, cut a rectangle of floral fabric the same as the bag front. Place the stitching and the fabric right-sides together, then sew around three edges, before turning over the top edge to neaten. Weave ribbon through the bag near to the top. Pull up the ribbon, and tie a bow.

Designed by Sue Cook

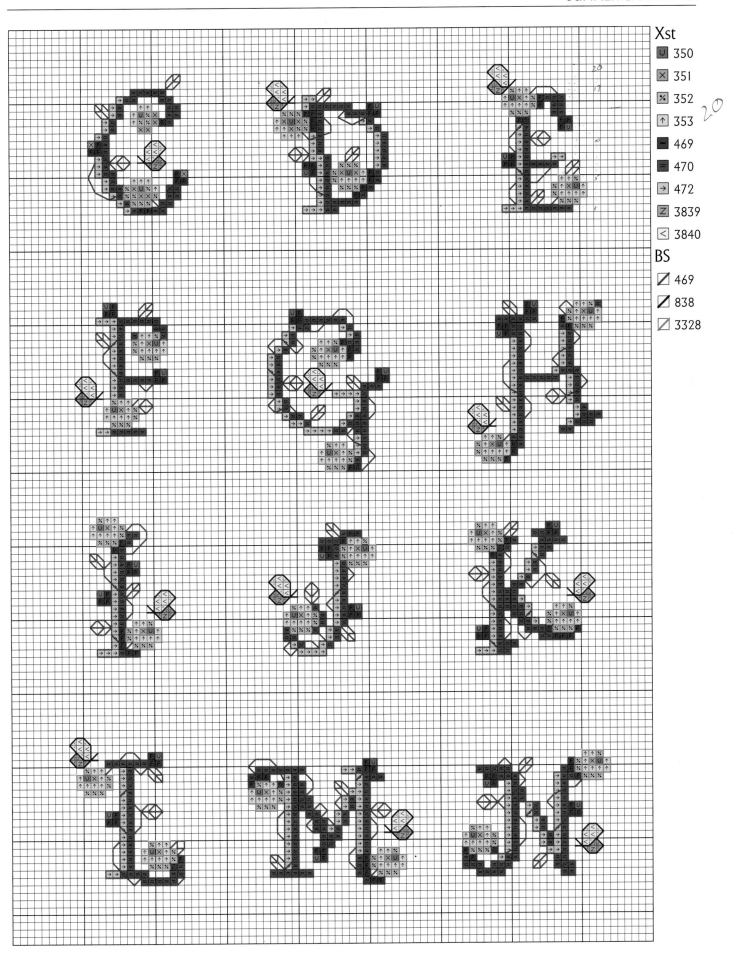

Xst
U 350
X 351
% 352
↑ 353
━ 469
═ 470
→ 472
Z 3839
< 3840

BS
◿ 469
◿ 838
◿ 3328

Xst
U	350
X	351
%	352
↑	353
■	469
▬	470
→	472
Z	3839
<	3840

BS
⧄	469
⧄	838
⧄	3328

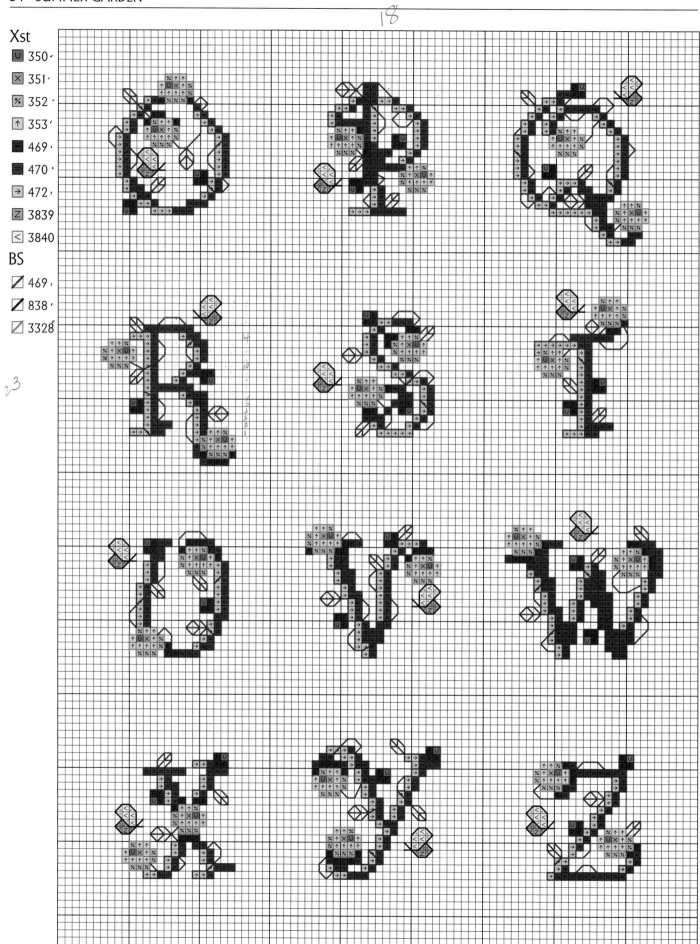

Spring Garden

Celebrate the season with this delightful alphabet of flowers and
butterflies designed in fresh spring colours

Designed by Helen Philipps

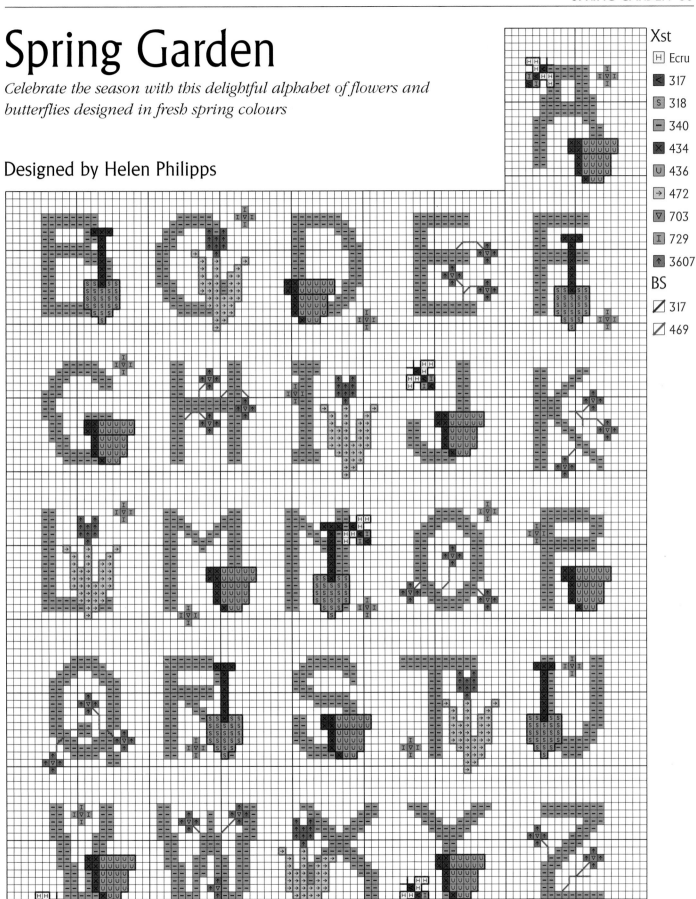

Xst	
H	Ecru
<	317
S	318
-	340
X	434
U	436
→	472
▽	703
I	729
↑	3607

BS	
╱	317
╱	469

Delft

Coordinate your dining table with this pretty alphabet inspired by Delft blue china

The napkin ring was made from 28 count cream linen, working each stitch over two thread of fabric. The napkin was made from white 14 count aida fabric, frayed at the edges. Both designs use DMC stranded cotton (floss), as listed in the key. The napkin ring was made from a strip of fabric large enough to fit around a napkin. Once the letter was stitched, the top and bottom edges were neatened, and then the fabric joined at the back to create a ring.

Designed by Lucie Heaton

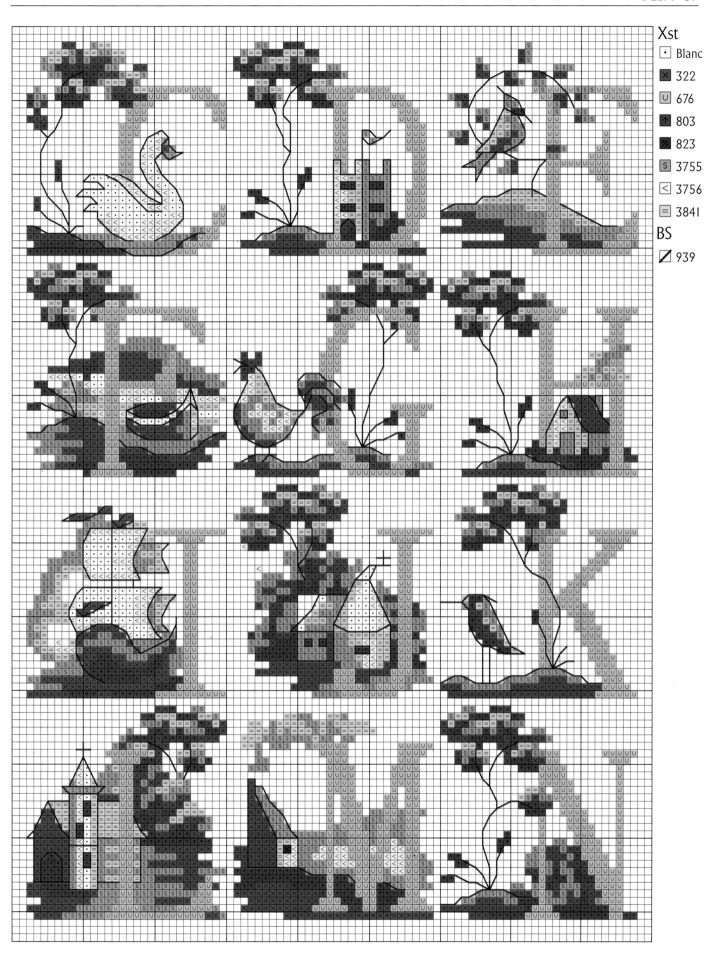

Xst

·	Blanc
✕	322
U	676
↑	803
▦	823
S	3755
<	3756
=	3841

BS

| ∕ | 939 |

Xst

· Blanc

× 322

U 676

↑ 803

✖ 823

S 3755

< 3756

= 3841

BS

╱ 939

Oriental

Capture the mysteries of the orient with this unusual alphabet inspired by the land of the rising sun

Designed by Claire Crompton

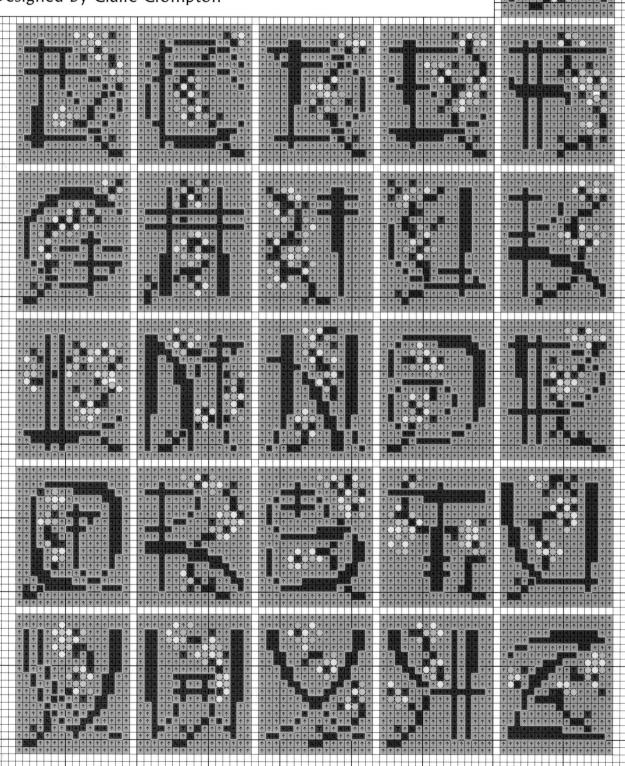

Xst
- T 700
- 991
- ↑ 993
- 3858

BS
- Gold

FK
- 819
- 899
- 3326

Wedding

Stitched into a keepsake, this ribbon alphabet embellished with hearts is a delightful way to commemorate the special day

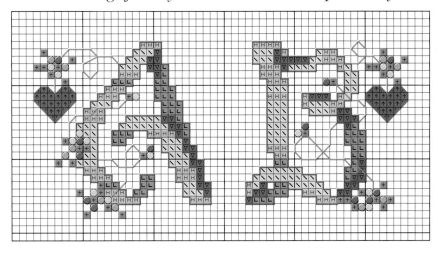

These delightful wedding gift bags were stitched on to white 14 count aida fabric using DMC stranded cotton (floss), as listed in the key. The designs were then made into gift bags, adding ribbon handles.

The letters from this alphabet could be made into a matching collection of stitched gifts for the happy couple, including a ring cushion, padded horseshoe and keepsake wedding album.

Designed by Claire Crompton

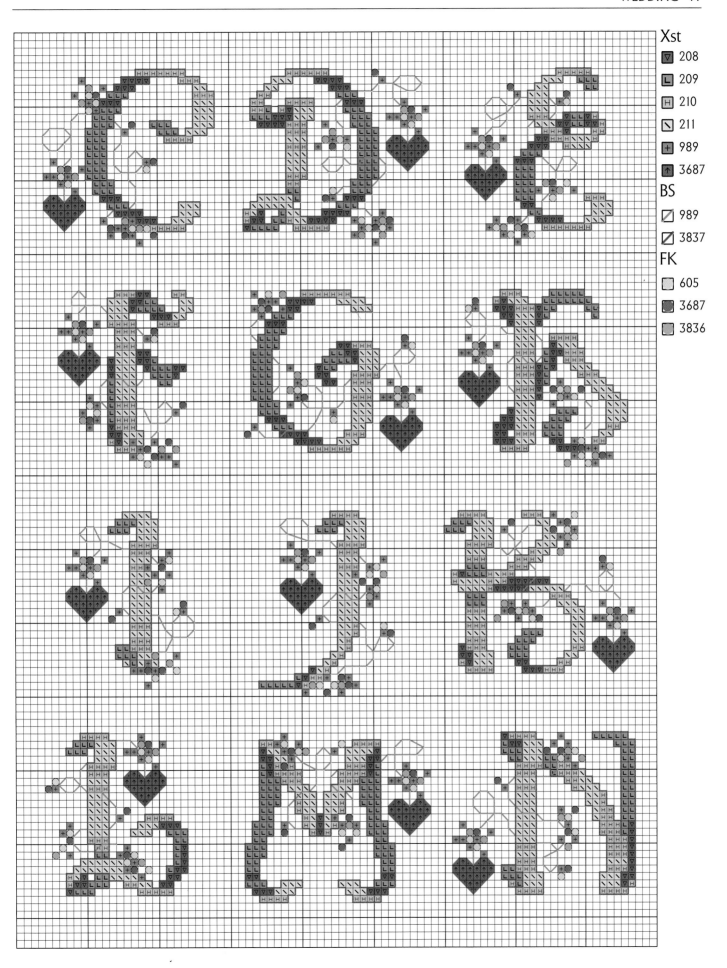

Xst
▽ 208
L 209
H 210
\ 211
+ 989
↑ 3687

BS
⊘ 989
⊘ 3837

FK
▢ 605
▢ 3687
▢ 3836

Xst

▽	208
L	209
H	210
\	211
+	989
▨	3687

BS

| ⧄ | 989 |
| ⧄ | 3837 |

FK

○	605
●	3687
○	3836

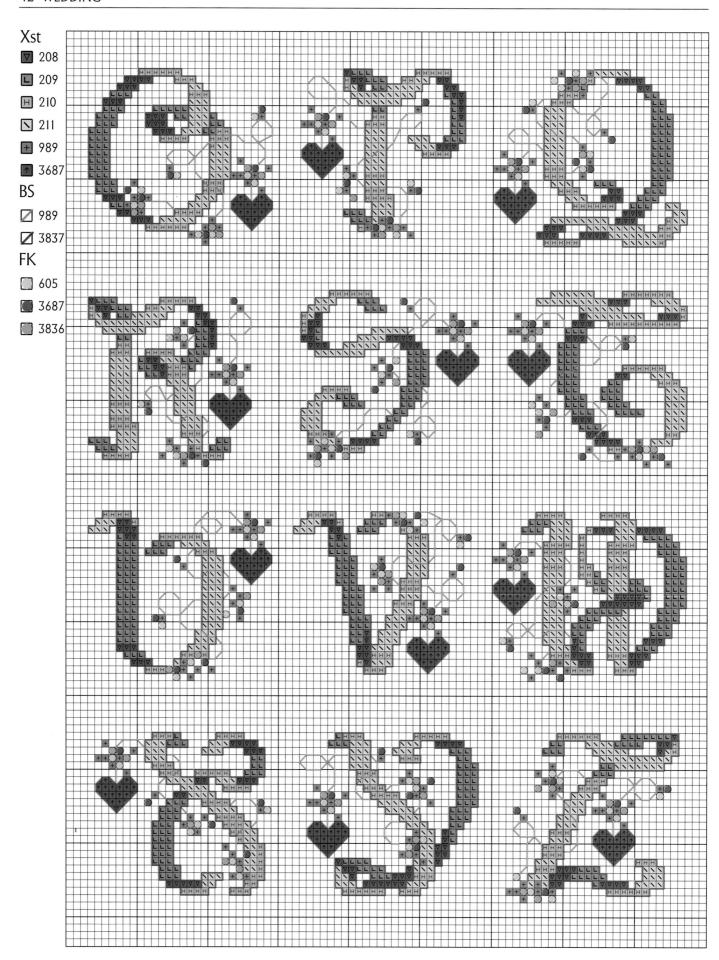

Hearts

Cupid's arrow is sure to catch the one you love with this heart alphabet designed in shades of pink and red

Designed by Maria Diaz

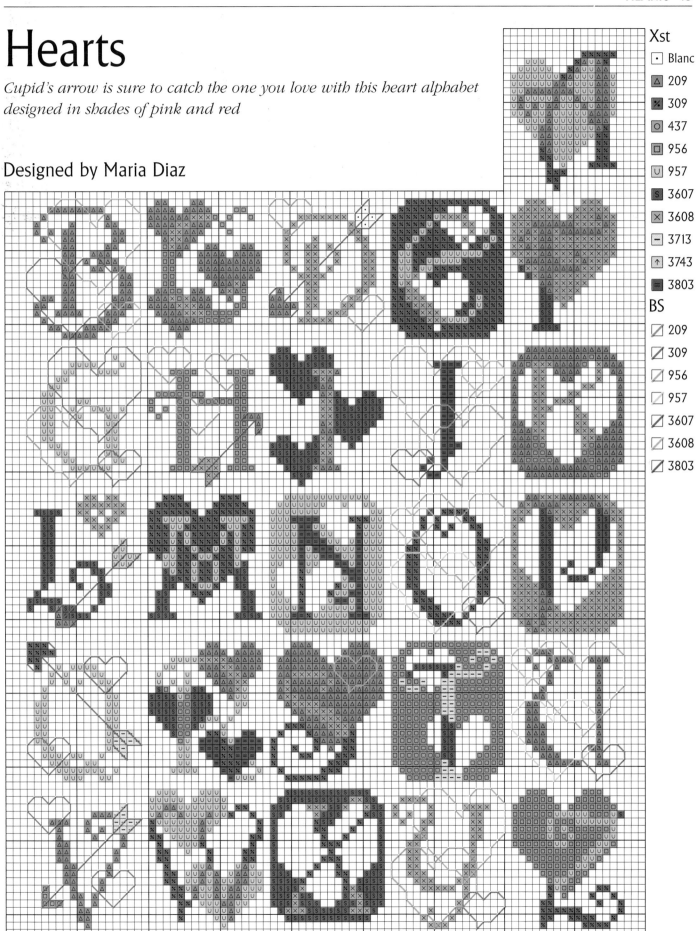

Xst

·	Blanc
△	209
%	309
⊙	437
▢	956
U	957
S	3607
×	3608
−	3713
↑	3743
=	3803

BS

╱	209
╱	309
╱	956
╱	957
╱	3607
╱	3608
╱	3803

Celtic

Adapted from Celtic art, this distinctive alphabet can be used to add initials to stationery and clothing

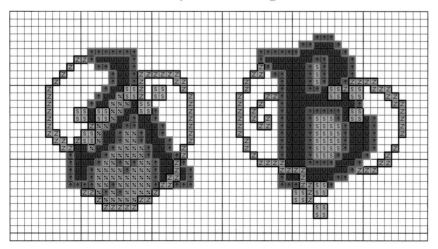

The gift card and address book initial were stitched on 28 count grey evenweave fabric, working each stitch on the chart over two threads of fabric, in the DMC stranded cotton (floss) colours listed in the key.

The letters from this alphabet could be used to monogram a dressing gown and slippers using waste canvas, or stitch the complete alphabet and make it into a sampler, cushion or stool cover.

Designed by Caroline Palmer

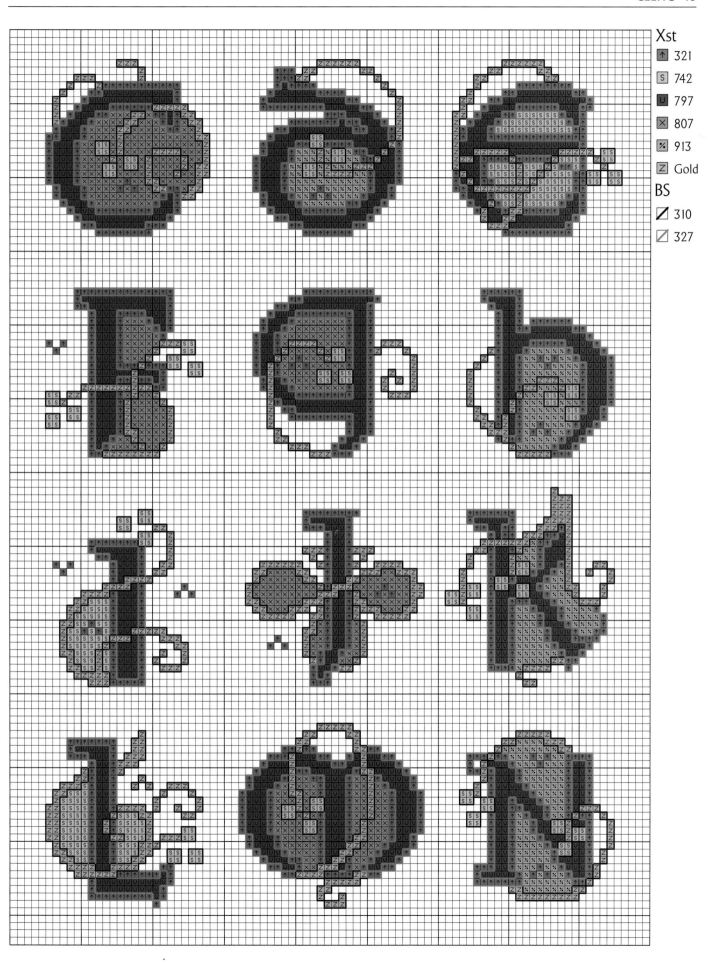

Xst

↑ 321
S 742
U 797
✕ 807
⁒ 913
Z Gold

BS

╱ 310
╱ 327

Xst

↑	321
S	742
U	797
X	807
⅗	913
Z	Gold

BS

◿	310
◿	327

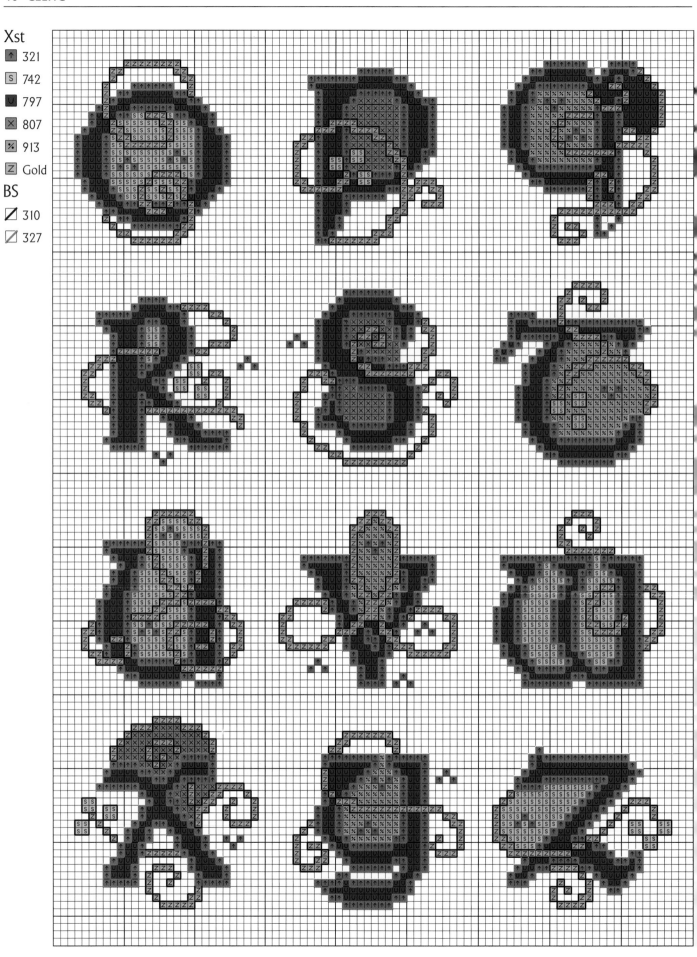

Native American

Capture the spirit of the Great Plains with this bold design, based on the traditional art and culture of Native Americans

Designed by Susan Penny

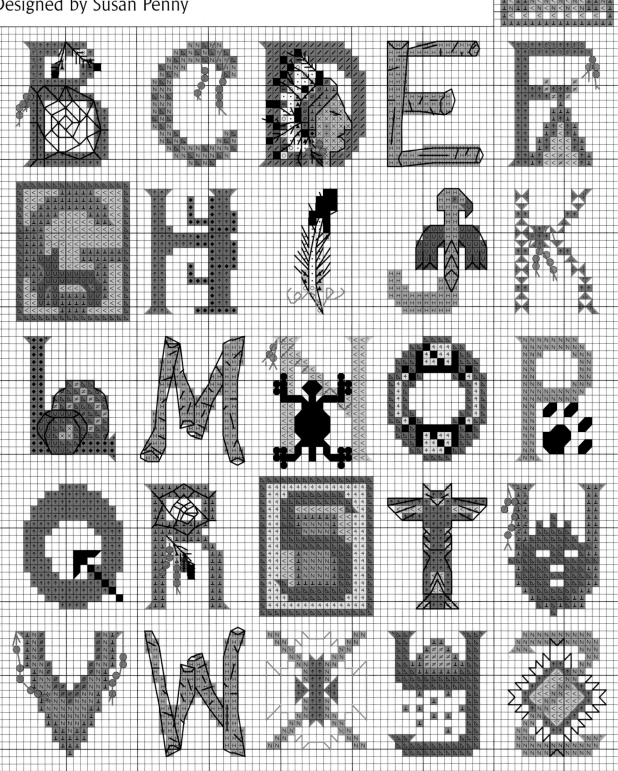

Xst

⊡	Blanc
⊍	301
■	310
⊟	414
▲	415
↑	666
4	677
◆	702
◹	720
✕	758
⊙	762
◪	798
N	907
◁	973
⊥	995
≠	996
⊞	3064
■	3371
⊘	3607
⊞	3778

BS

⧄	301
⧄	310
⧄	666
⧄	995

FK

●	310
■	666
■	995

Ships

Sailing ships, liners and boats from many far off lands are featured in this maritime alphabet

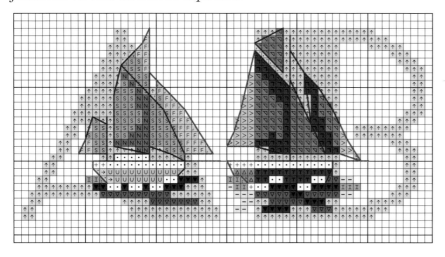

The initials were stitched on to the hand towel and flannel using waste canvas, working each stitch on the chart over two threads of canvas, in the DMC stranded cotton (floss) colours listed in the key. To stitch each initial, tack a piece of waste canvas on to the towel or flannel, then stitch over the threads of the waste canvas to form the stitches. When the cross stitch is complete, spray the canvas lightly with water, and then use tweezers to remove the canvas threads.

Designed by Claire Crompton

Xst

· Blanc
■ 312
< 415
S 422
Z 434
H 436
→ 727
C 738
= 739
I 762
924
4 926
930
▽ 931
I 932
> 950
N 3045
F 3047
∩ 3325
- 3753
T 3777
△ 3778
◛ 3779
U 3820
Σ 3830
↑ 3841
▧ 3858
◲ 3859
+ 3866

BS

⟋ 632
⟋ 938

Xst

·	Blanc
⌐	312
<	415
S	422
▧	434
H	436
→	727
C	738
=	739
I	762
✕	924
◀	926
▼	930
▽	931
I	932
>	950
N	3045
F	3047
∩	3325
−	3753
T	3777
△	3778
╲	3779
U	3820
Σ	3830
↑	3841
⌐	3858
◁	3859
+	3866

BS

╱	632
╱	938

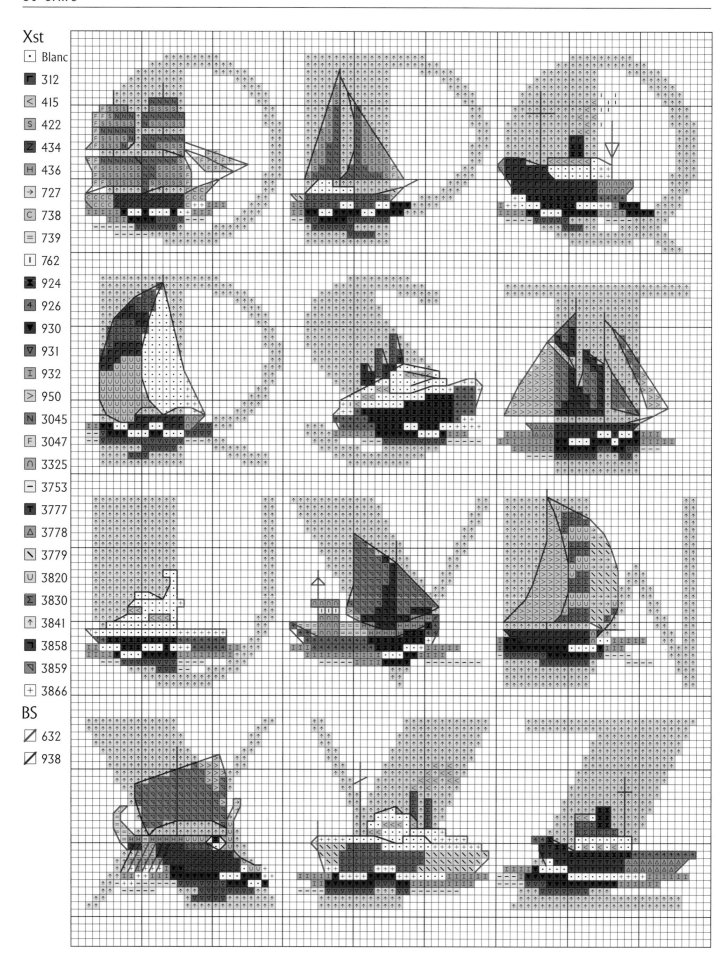

Nautical

This nautical alphabet of anchors and flags is sure to please both seafarers and landlubbers alike

Designed by Susan Penny

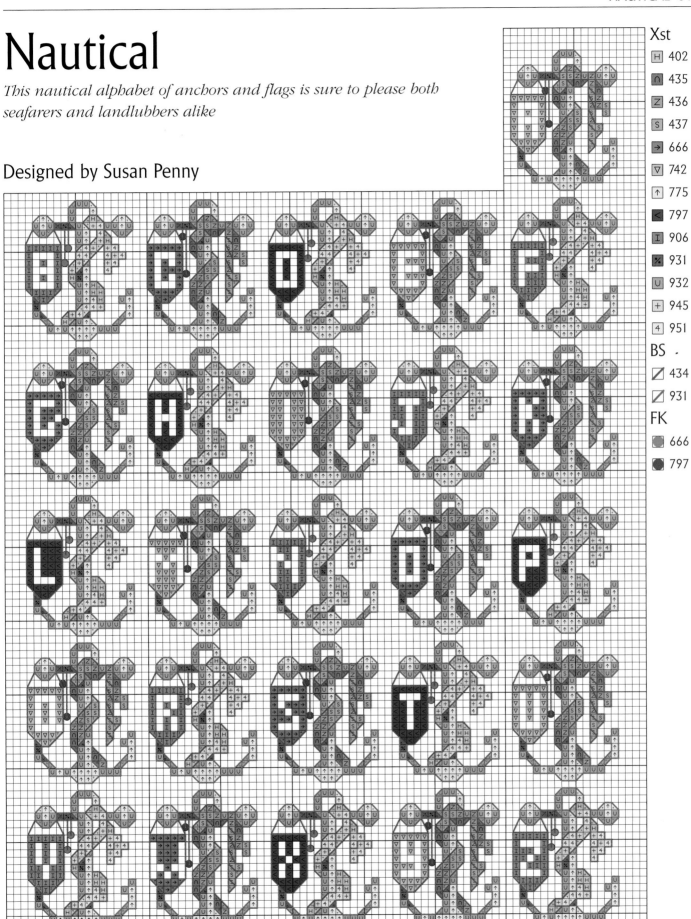

Xst

H	402
∩	435
Z	436
S	437
→	666
▽	742
↑	775
◄	797
I	906
%	931
U	932
+	945
4	951

BS -

⁄	434
⁄	931

FK

●	666
●	797

Christmas

*Send a message of peace and love this Christmas with letters
taken from this charming seasonal alphabet*

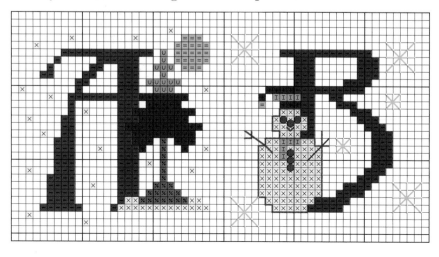

The stocking top was made from 32 count ecru linen. Each stitch on the chart was worked over two threads of fabric, in the DMC stranded cotton (floss) colours listed in the key. Make a pattern of your top, twice the width of your stocking. Cut two shapes from linen, then sew the fabric pieces together, along the top and bottom edges. Turn to the right side, then sew the open ends together to form a ring. Attach the top to the stocking and decorate with bells.

Designed by Helen Philipps

Xst
⊠ Ecru
▬ 221
↑ 317
⊠ 420
→ 422
+ 501
Ｕ 503
< 778
Ｉ 932
= 977
S 3799

BS
╱ 414
╱ 501
╱ 742
╱ 3799

FK
● 221
● 317

Xst

- ☒ Ecru
- ▬ 221
- ↑ 317
- ▨ 420
- → 422
- ▦ 501
- U 503
- < 778
- I 932
- = 977
- S 3799

BS

- ◿ 414
- ◿ 501
- ◿ 742
- ◿ 3799

FK

- ● 221
- ● 317

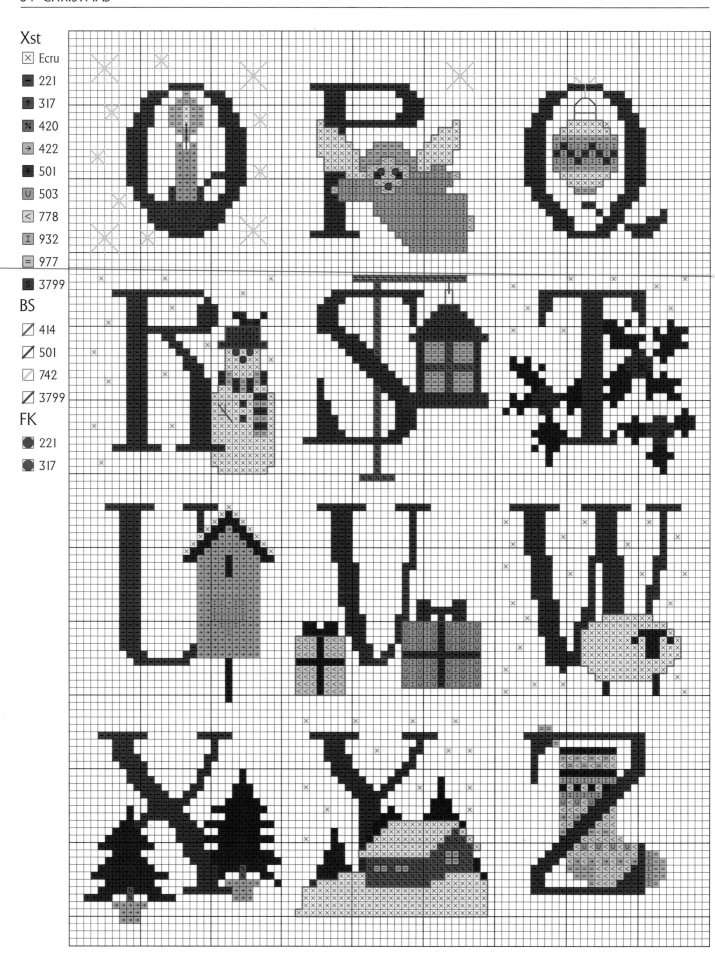

Christmas Bows

This attractive alphabet in red and green, decorated with mistletoe and red bows, is sure to become a favourite when stitching for Christmas

Designed by Caroline Palmer

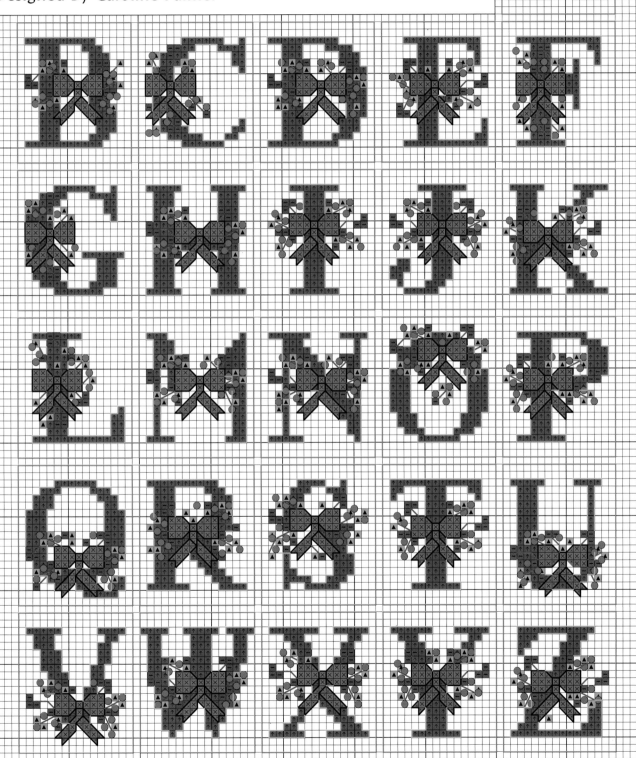

Xst
- ■ 310
- 498
- ✕ 666
- ─ 700
- ▲ 704

BS
- ╱ 310
- ╱ 666
- ╱ 700
- ╱ Gold

FK
- ⬡ 666

Cottages

Clarice Cliff's imaginative pottery designs have inspired this
pretty alphabet, which has many uses from cards to coasters

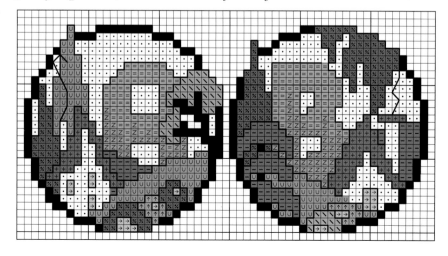

The key ring and pot top were stitched on 14 count white aida fabric, in the DMC stranded cotton (floss) colours listed in the key.

Letters from this alphabet could be stitched into gift cards for many different occasions; from birthdays to house warming messages. Stitch individual letters, or two together to make a larger card. The round shape of the letters makes them useful for mounting in coasters and luggage tags.

Designed by Sue Cook

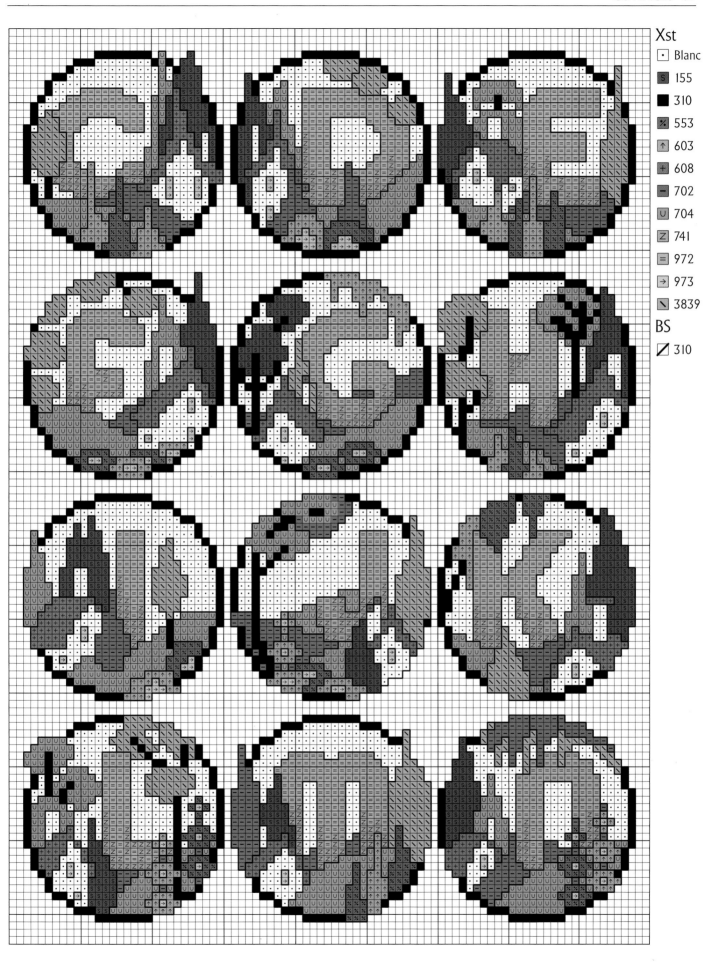

Xst
⊡ Blanc
▣ 155
■ 310
▨ 553
↑ 603
+ 608
− 702
Ⓤ 704
Ⓩ 741
= 972
→ 973
◥ 3839
BS
⧄ 310

Xst

·	Blanc
S	155
■	310
%	553
↑	603
+	608
−	702
U	704
Z	741
=	972
→	973
\	3839

BS

⁄	310

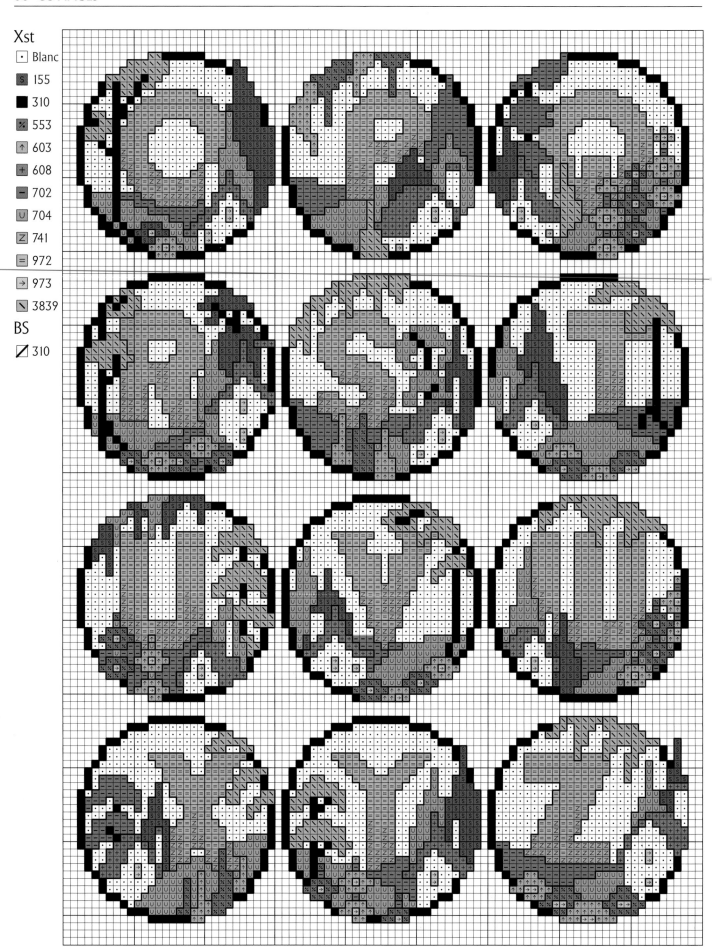

Scripts

These useful script alphabets can be used to personalize greetings cards and samplers

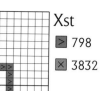

Xst
> 798
× 3832

Designed by Susan Penny

Dinosaurs

Fierce and friendly dinosaurs have been stitched on this useful bag for storing comics, art material or as a pyjama case

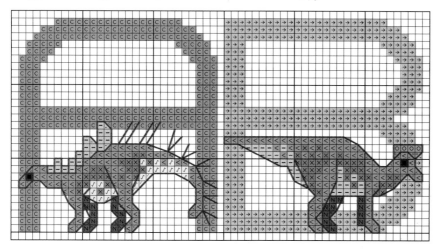

The letters were stitched on 14 count white aida fabric, in the DMC stranded cotton (floss) colours listed in the key.

The bag front, back and flap should be cut from one piece of 14 count white aida fabric. Fold the fabric into a bag, and then sew the side seams together on the wrong side. The bag can then be lined with cotton fabric, and the flap edged with green binding. A loop and button should be stitched on to the flap for fastening.

Designed by Claire Crompton

Xst

F	168
◥	318
●	413
Z	414
↑	415
C	452
→	453
I	471
✖	501
▽	502
U	503
N	611
✕	612
<	613
⌐	762
■	898
I	928
=	950
▪	3011
Σ	3012
∩	3013
−	3047
▬	3051
○	3064
▪	3362
◲	3363
◺	3364
⊥	3772
+	3813
▼	3858

BS

| ╱ | 898 |

Xst

F	168
◣	318
◆	413
Z	414
↑	415
C	452
→	453
I	471
✖	501
▽	502
U	503
N	611
✕	612
<	613
✓	762
■	898
I	928
=	950
■	3011
Σ	3012
∩	3013
−	3047
▼	3051
◯	3064
■	3362
▮	3363
�	3364
⊥	3772
+	3813
▼	3858

BS

| ╱ | 898 |

Rockets and Planets

Reach for the stars and beyond with this colourful space alphabet featuring rockets and planets

Designed by Lucie Heaton

Xst

·	Blanc
↑	155
I	162
S	307
H	333
O	444
▽	498
↓	597
Z	606
F	704
+	740
%	742
✕	797
N	907
=	996
→	3801
U	3809
4	3843

BS

◣	Blanc
◢	906

Herbs and Flowers

Nasturtiums, forget-me-nots and borage are just some of the flowers and herbs mixed together to create this floral alphabet

The note book initial and apron pocket were stitched on 28 count antique white linen, working each stitch on the chart over two threads of fabric, in the DMC stranded cotton (floss) colours listed in the key.

Cut the apron pocket from linen. Neaten across the top edge before attaching it to the apron at the sides and bottom. Wrap the letter for the note book around a square of firm card. Stitch piping around the edge, then glue it to the note book front.

Designed by Anne Wilson

Xst

N	154
H	208
I	210
→	326
Z	340
✱	367
←	704
+	741
×	743
∩	827
<	961
⁒	962
=	963
−	972
4	996
▲	3347
S	3706
↑	3716
U	3801
F	3863

BS

╱	154
╱	208
╱	318
╱	319
╱	326
╱	704
╱	721
╱	741
╱	962
╱	3801
╱	3863

FK

●	154
●	319
●	743
●	3863

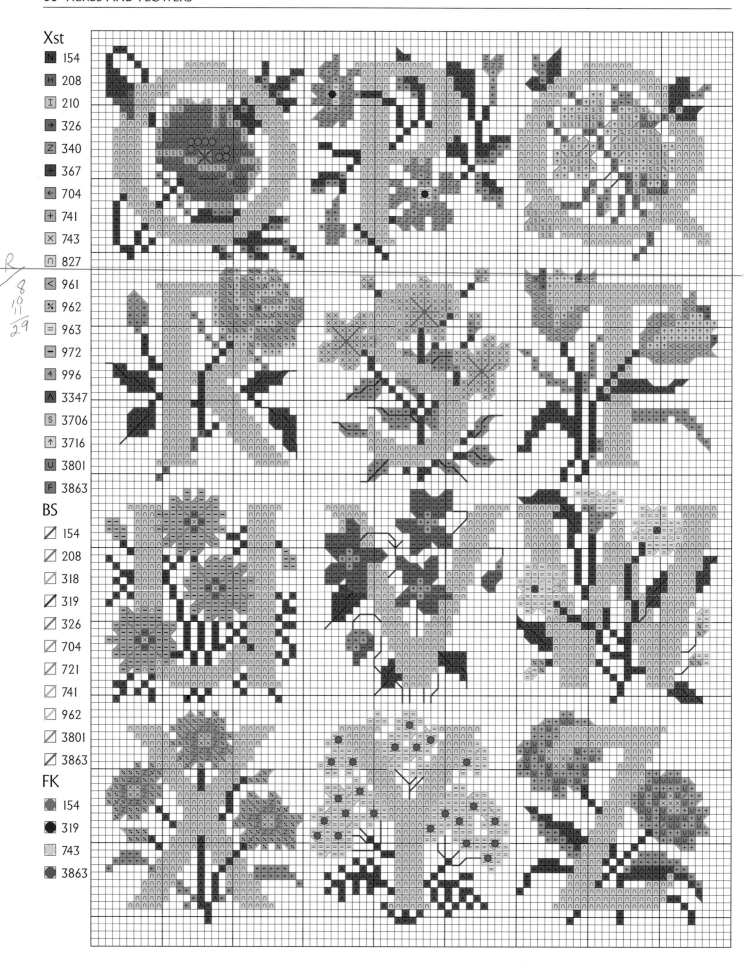

Xst

N	154
H	208
I	210
→	326
Z	340
▦	367
←	704
+	741
✕	743
∩	827
<	961
%	962
=	963
-	972
4	996
∧	3347
S	3706
↑	3716
U	3801
F	3863

BS

╱	154
╱	208
╱	318
╱	319
╱	326
╱	704
╱	721
╱	741
╱	962
╱	3801
╱	3863

FK

●	154
●	319
●	743
●	3863

Bees

Shades of aqua and green have been used to create this buzzy alphabet featuring honey bees busily collecting pollen

Designed by Lesley Teare

Xst	
·	Blanc
✕	164
■	310
✓	725
V	772
S	783
U	907
*	913
▲	924
↑	955

BS

╱	310
╱	701

FK

●	310

Baby

Baby will love to wear this fun bib decorated with a sail boat
and train, which is sure to keep him clean at meal time

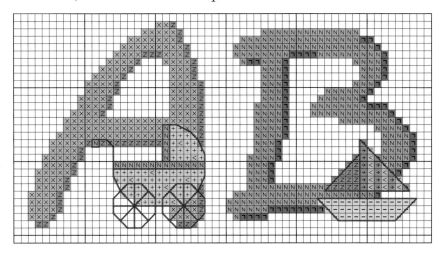

This ready-made baby bib in a shade of pale lemon has a white 14 count aida panel at the bottom for cross stitching. The letters taken from the nursery alphabet were stitched using DMC stranded cotton (floss), as listed in the key.

You could make your own bib, or add an aida panel to the bottom of a plain ready-made baby bib, finishing the edges with matching binding tape.

Designed by Maria Diaz

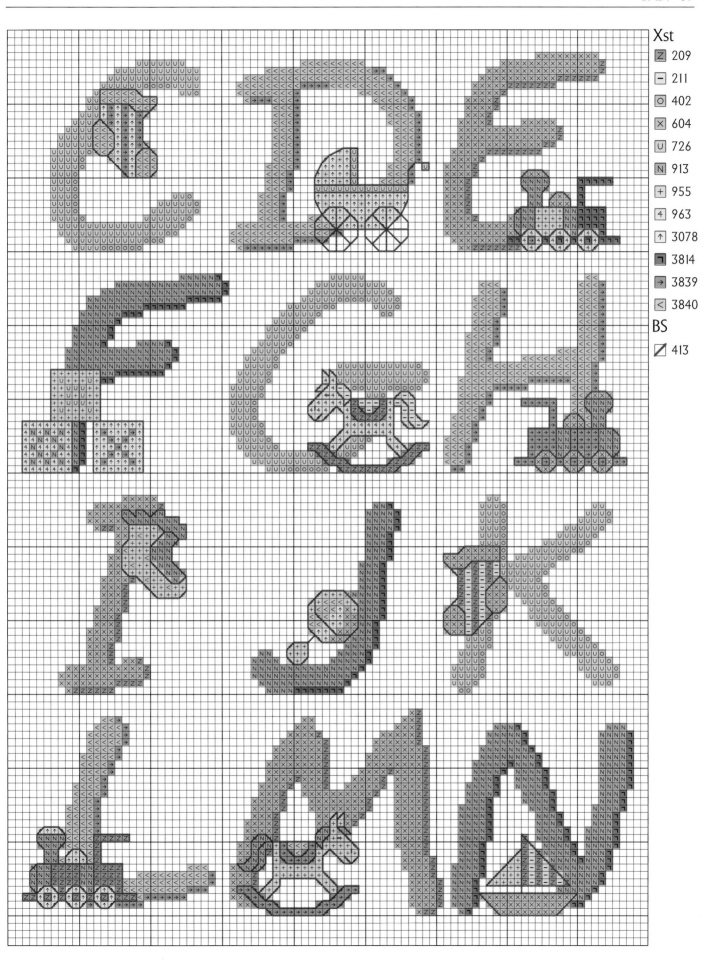

Xst

Z	209	
−	211	
O	402	
X	604	
U	726	
N	913	
+	955	
4	963	
↑	3078	
⌐	3814	
→	3839	
<	3840	

BS

∕	413

Xst

Z	209
-	211
O	402
X	604
U	726
N	913
+	955
4	963
↑	3078
◣	3814
→	3839
<	3840

BS

╱	413

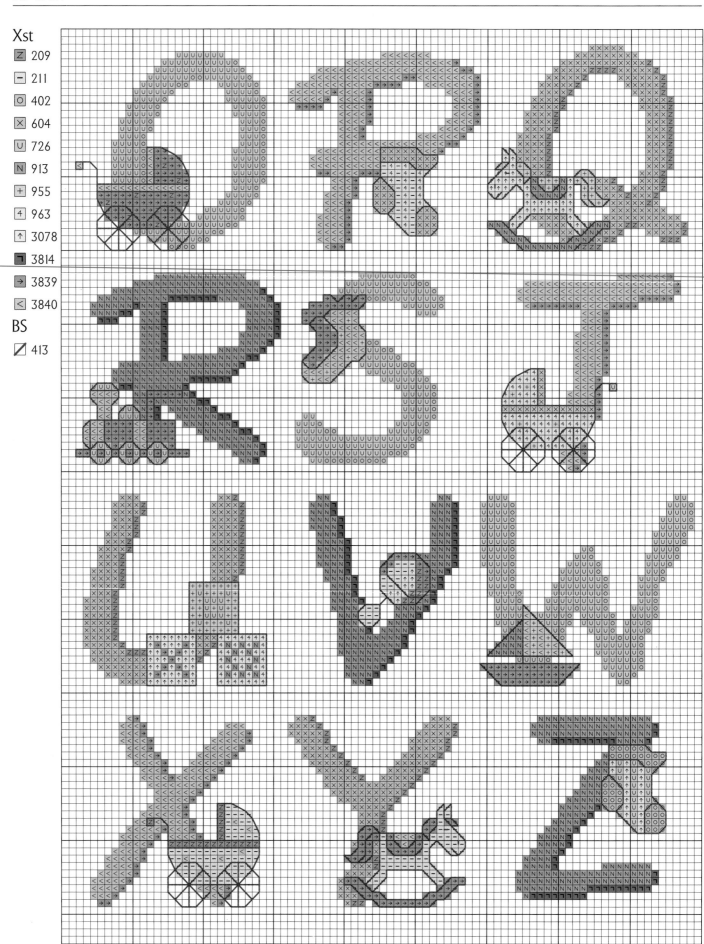

Nursery

*Bright primary colours have been used to design this fun nursery
alphabet which could be used for cards, or stitched as a sampler*

Designed by Susan Penny

Xst	
·	Blanc
■	310
–	318
◈	434
⚡	519
↑	666
◆	703
<	725
→	727
◣	729
←	747
□	907
∨	972
⊥	996
s	3706
▽	3801
т	3821
⌐	3838

BS	
╱	310

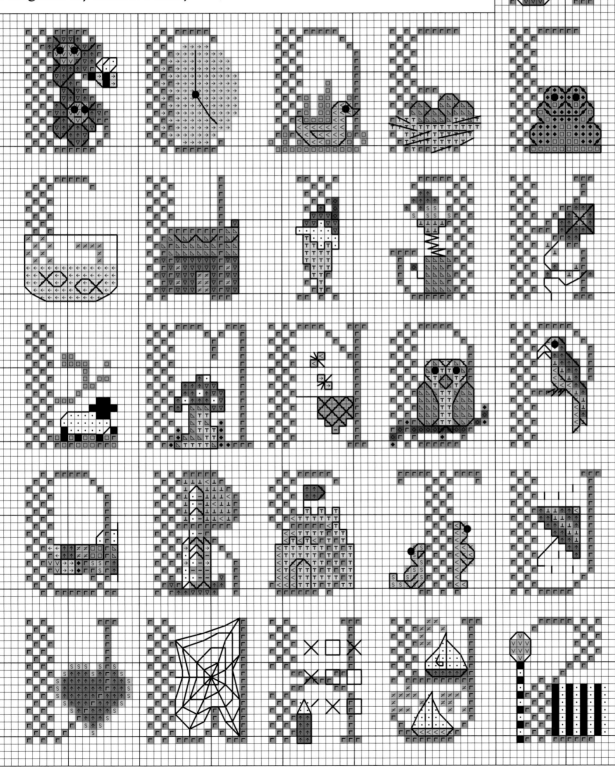

Folk Art

*Simple images of gingerbread men, apples and sheep have
been used to create this imaginative folk art alphabet*

The initials in the framed picture and attached
to the wooden spoon were stitched on 32
count ecru linen, working each stitch over
two threads of fabric, in the DMC stranded
cotton (floss) colours listed in the key.

The spoon was made by cutting two
circles of linen, which were then sewn
together, right sides facing, leaving a small
gap for turning. Once turned and stuffed the
gap was sewn up, and the decoration
attached to the spoon with ribbon.

Designed by Maria Diaz

Xst
S	349
X	351
↑	353
✚	699
N	701
<	704
4	743
+	745
U	783
Z	825
O	826
-	827

BS
◹	3021

Xst

S	349
X	351
↑	353
▓	699
N	701
<	704
4	743
+	745
U	783
Z	825
O	826
-	827

BS

| / | 3021 |

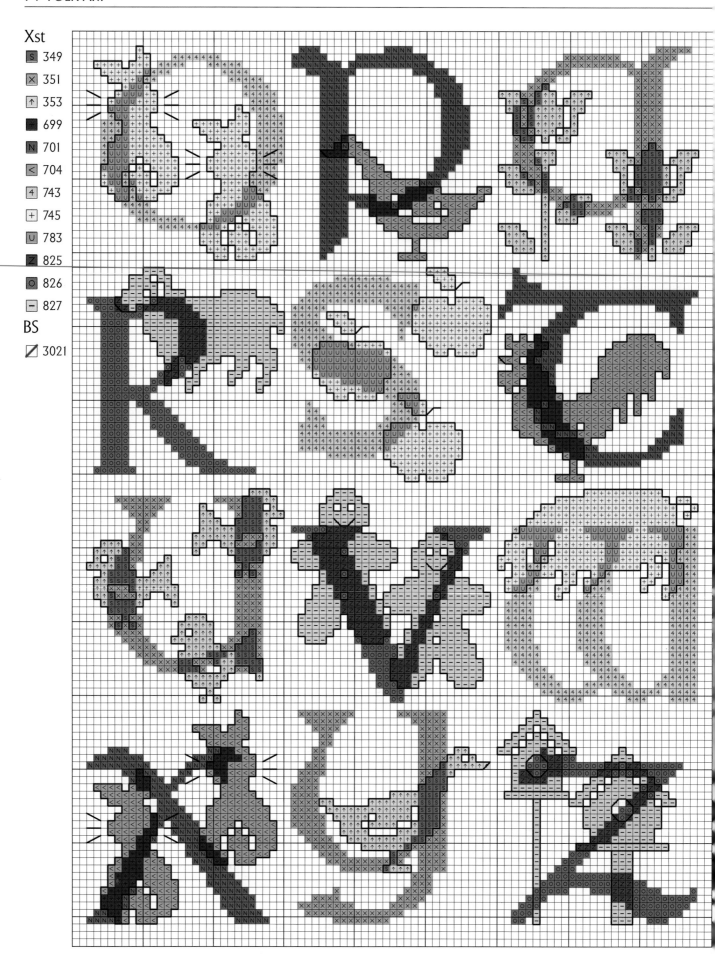

Scripts

Less ornate alphabets have many uses in cross stitch designs, from adding names and dates to samplers to monogramming clothing

Designed by Susan Penny

	Xst
U	208
=	209
X	3838
−	3839
S	3840
BS	
⁄	208

11 spaces

Egyptian

*Artifacts from the ancient land of the Pharaohs have inspired
this ornate, richly embellished alphabet*

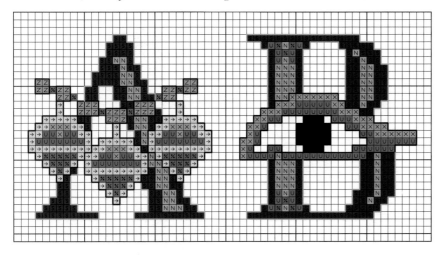

The initials used to decorate the compact lid
and mirror case were stitched on to 32 count
cream linen, working each stitch on the chart
over two threads of fabric, in the DMC
stranded cotton (floss) colours listed in the
key. Gold thread was used on the design to
give the letters a rich antique feel.

After stitching, the fabric was cut to size,
and frayed at the edges, before attaching
with small stitches to the mirror case.

Designed by Caroline Palmer

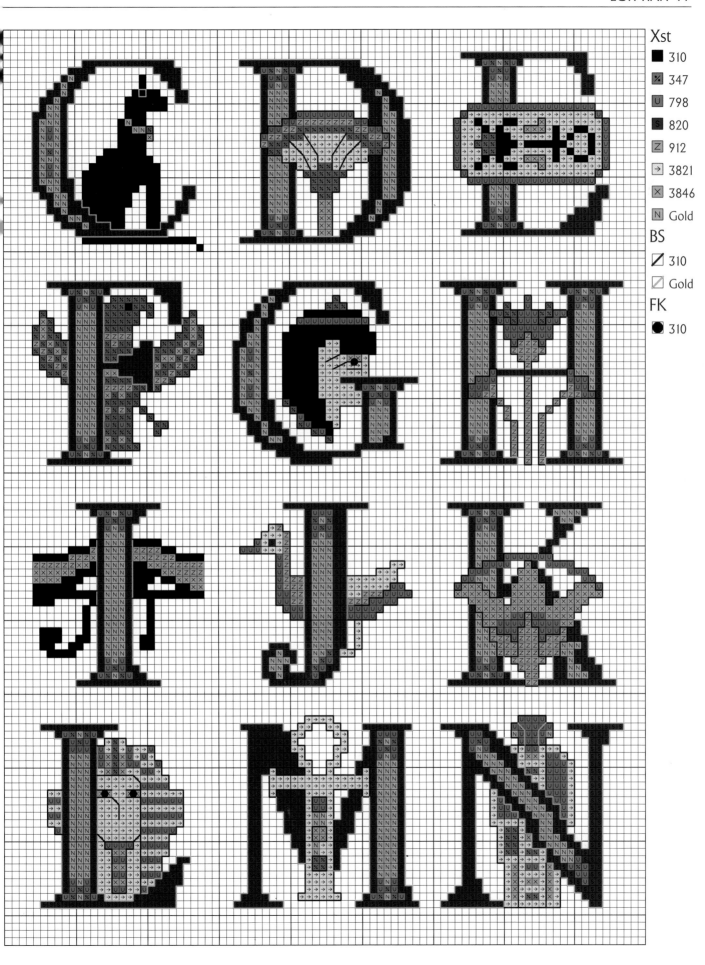

Xst
- ■ 310
- ⊠ 347
- ⊍ 798
- ▣ 820
- ⊠ 912
- → 3821
- ⊠ 3846
- Ⓝ Gold

BS
- ╱ 310
- ╱ Gold

FK
- ● 310

Xst
- ■ 310
- ▨ 347
- U 798
- ▦ 820
- Z 912
- → 3821
- ✕ 3846
- N Gold

BS
- ╱ 310
- ╱ Gold

FK
- ● 310

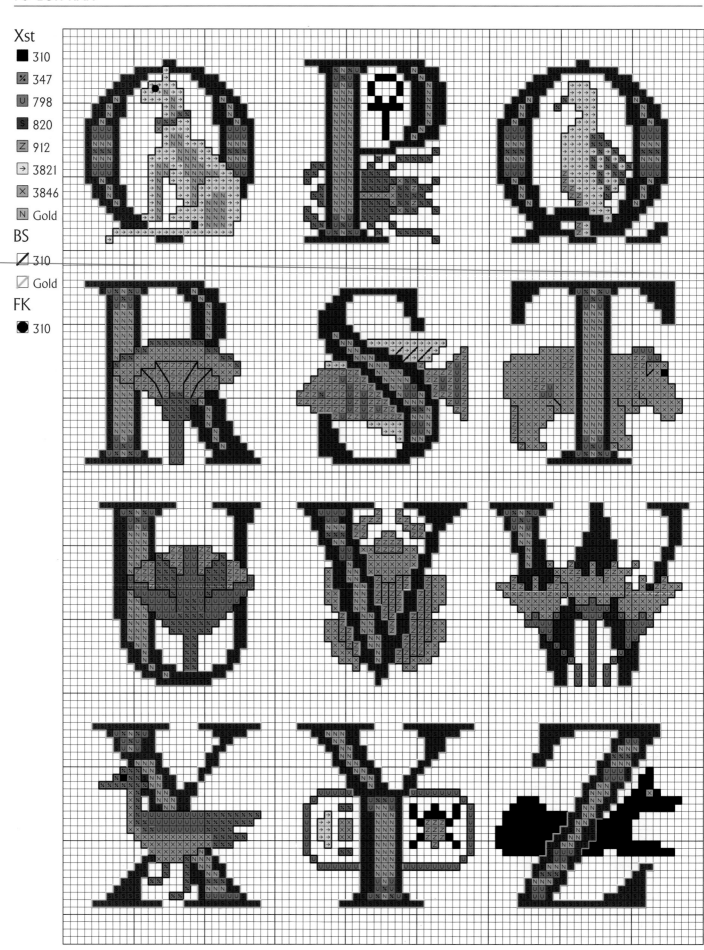

Heraldic

For many hundreds of years shields have been used to represent family history. This heraldic alphabet is a nice way to display your family name

Designed by Maria Diaz

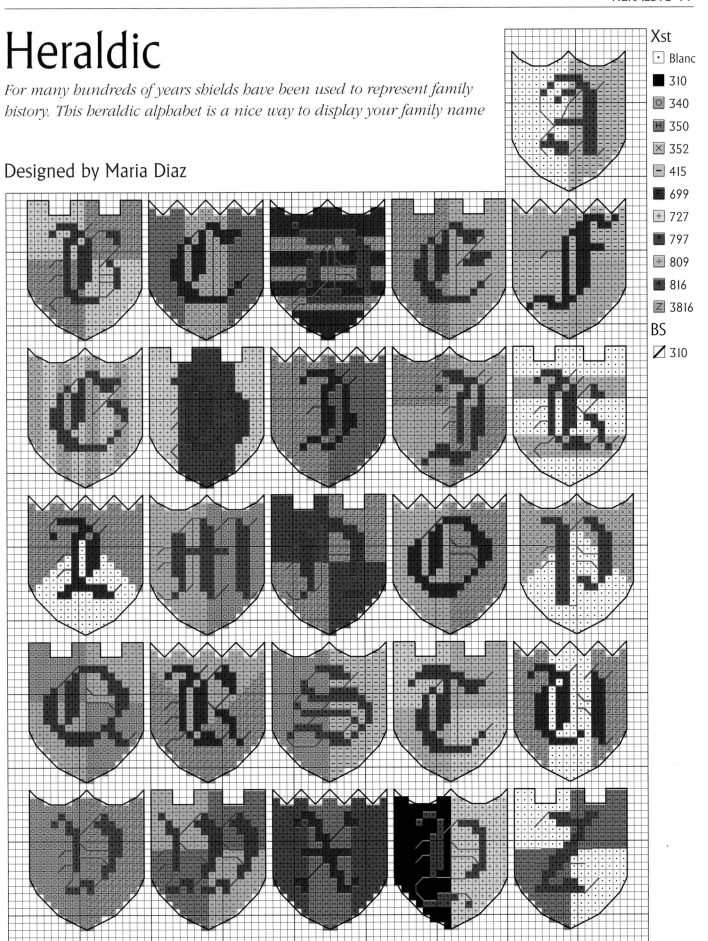

Xst
- · Blanc
- ■ 310
- ○ 340
- H 350
- ✕ 352
- − 415
- ■ 699
- + 727
- ↑ 797
- ÷ 809
- ⊞ 816
- Z 3816

BS
- ╱ 310

Noah's Ark

Noah's Ark has always been a favourite amongst children, so this cute alphabet is a lovely way to decorate a child's sun hat

The design was stitched on to 28 count pale pink evenweave, working each stitch on the chart over two threads of fabric, in the DMC stranded cotton (floss) colours listed in the key. The hat badge was made by placing the completed stitching over a padded circle of card. Piping was then stitched around the edge, and the back covered with a circle of cotton fabric. Decorate with ribbon roses and then stitch a pin on to the back of the badge to attach it to the hat.

Designed by Maria Diaz

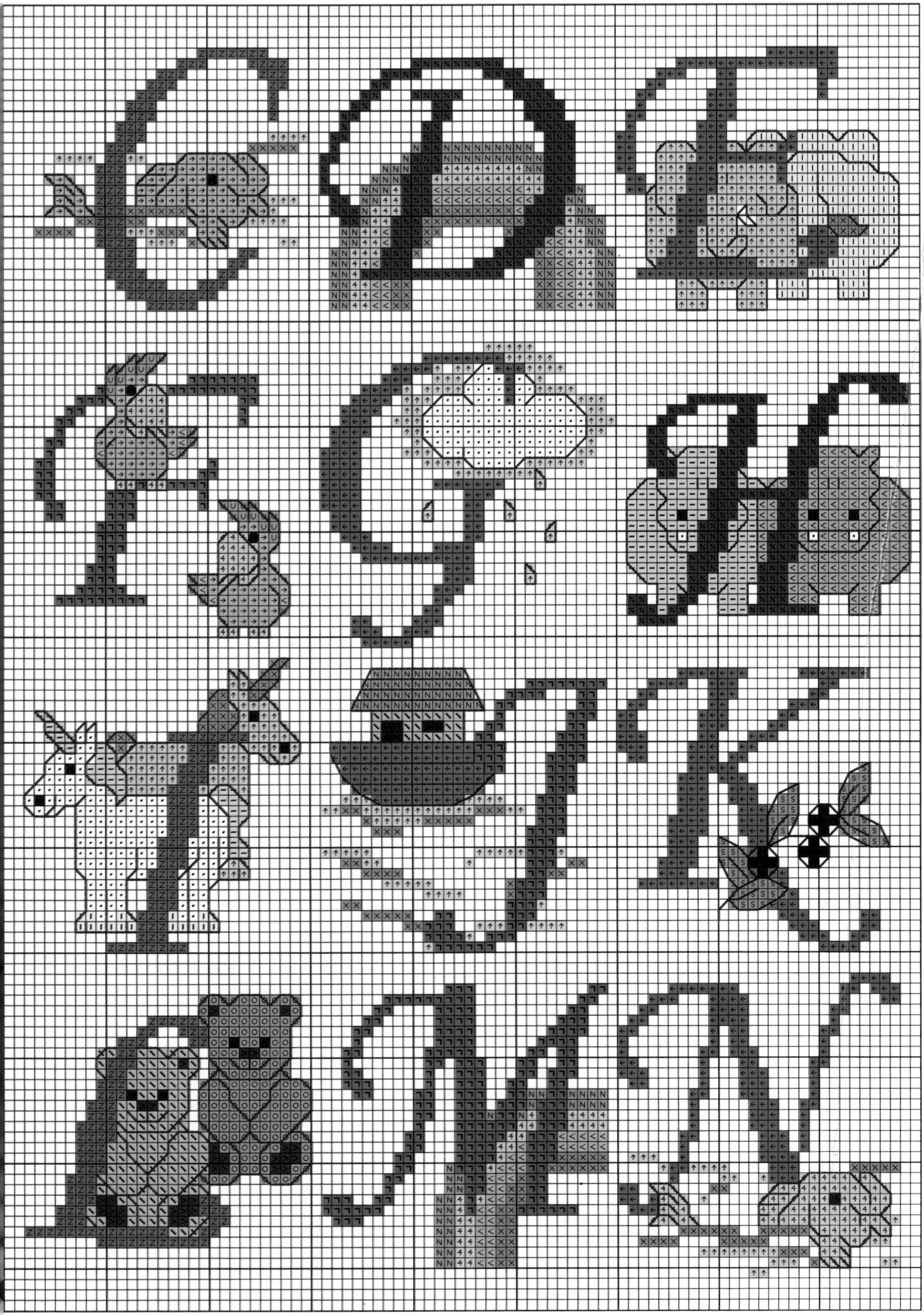

Xst

Symbol	Colour
·	Blanc
■	154
∩	209
–	211
⊠	333
◀	347
▶	433
O	436
<	604
S	704
╲	738
4	744
I	762
⌉	798
X	799
↑	800
→	954
U	996
N	3712
Z	3850

BS

Symbol	Colour
╱	154

Xst

·	Blanc
H	154
⌒	209
−	211
▨	333
←	347
＞	433
O	436
＜	604
S	704
＼	738
4	744
I	762
⌐	798
✕	799
↑	800
→	954
U	996
N	3712
Z	3850

BS

⁄	154

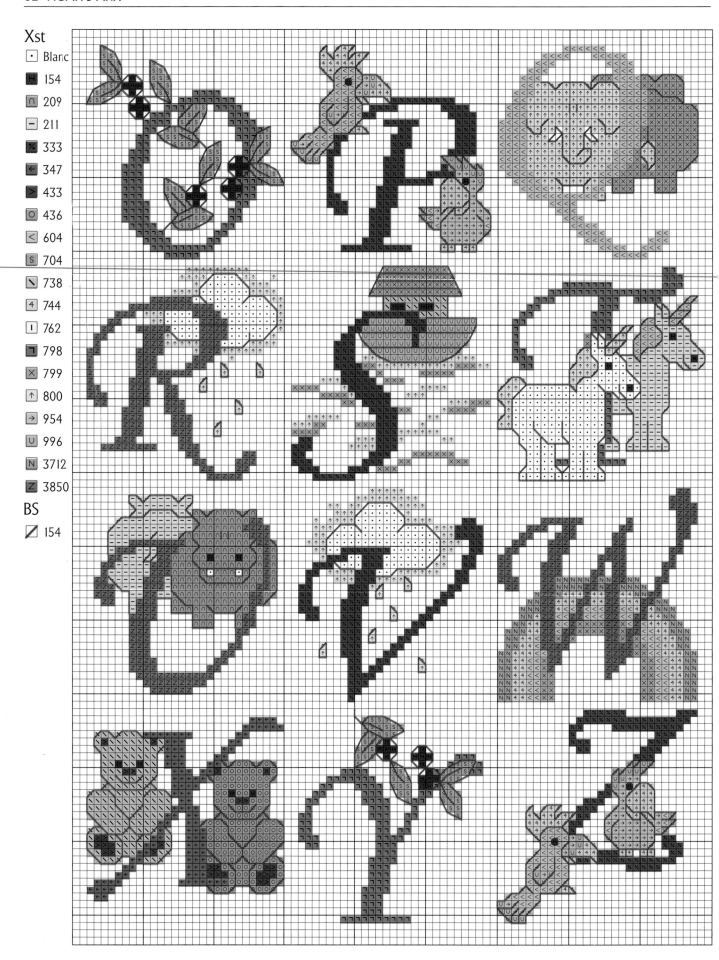

Bugs and Beetles

This fun alphabet crawling with caterpillars, beetles and ladybirds
would look great stitched up into a child's cot quilt

Designed by Maria Diaz

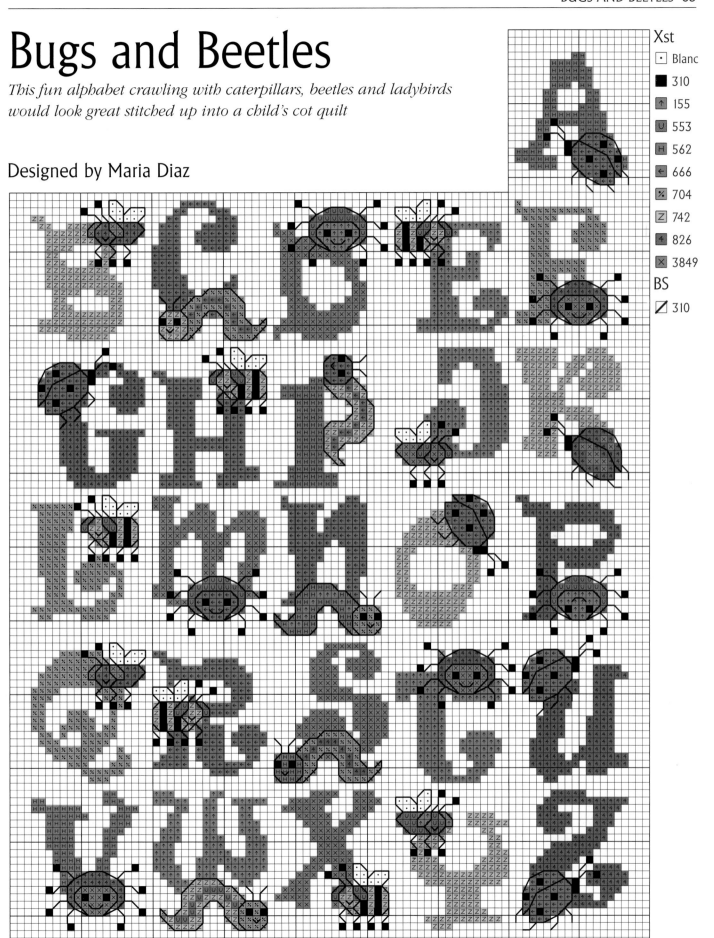

Xst	
⊡	Blanc
■	310
↑	155
U	553
H	562
←	666
⁒	704
Z	742
4	826
✕	3849

BS

╱	310

Flower Garden

For garden lovers this alphabet is a delight, with every letter featuring a different flower – from Azaleas to Zinnias

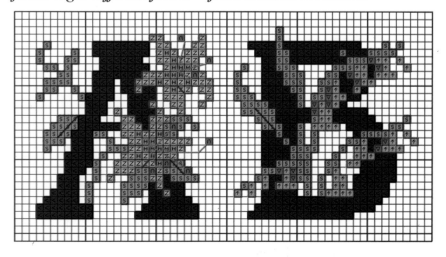

The cards were stitched on cream 28 count aida fabric, working each stitch on the chart over two threads of fabric, and using DMC stranded cotton (floss), as listed in the key. The flowers featured are: Azalea, Bluebell, Clematis, Daffodil, Edelweiss, Fuchsia, Geranium, Hollyhock, Iris, Japonica, Kaffir Lily, Lily, Morning Glory, Nasturtium, Oriental Poppy, Pansy, Quince, Rose, Sweet Pea, Trumpet Flower, Urn Plant, Vinca, Wisteria, Xmas Rose, Yellow Daisy and Zinnia.

Designed by Caroline Palmer

Xst

·	Blanc
−	208
⁒	210
■	310
=	352
U	603
✕	605
H	721
Z	722
F	725
→	727
▽	826
S	989
↑	3325
◣	3362
+	3801
∩	3829

BS

╱	300
╱	310
╱	336
╱	327
╱	815
╱	890
╱	3829

Xst

- · Blanc
- − 208
- ⁒ 210
- ■ 310
- ＝ 352
- U 603
- ⊠ 605
- H 721
- Z 722
- E 725
- → 727
- ▽ 826
- S 989
- ↑ 3325
- ◄ 3362
- + 3801
- ∩ 3829

BS

- ⊘ 300
- ⊘ 310
- ⊘ 336
- ⊘ 327
- ⊘ 815
- ⊘ 890
- ⊘ 3829

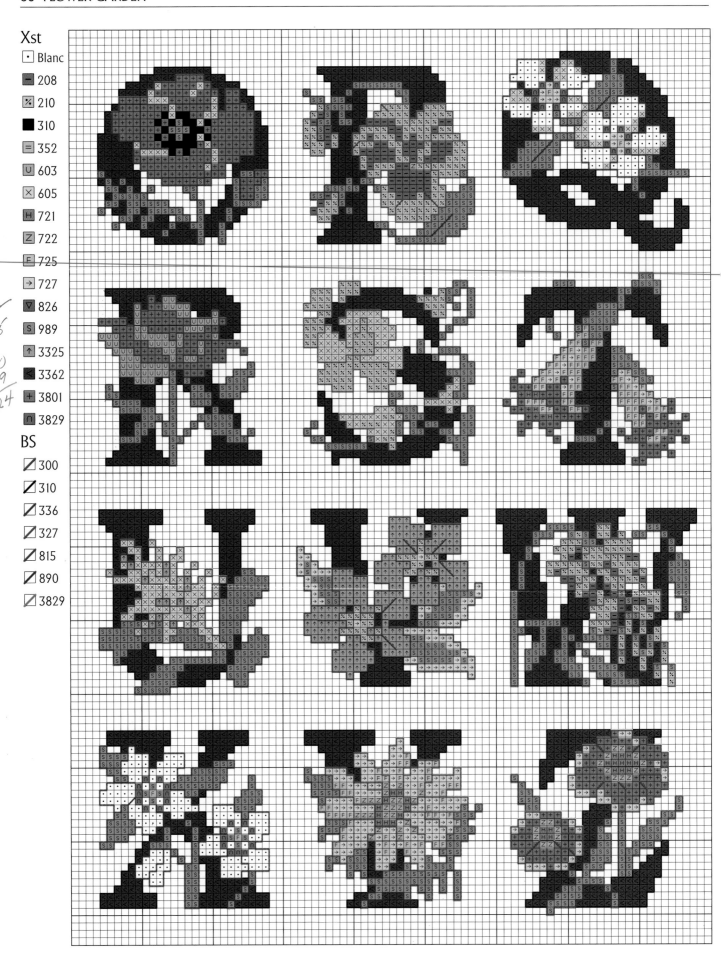

Butterflies

This charming alphabet with butterflies fluttering playfully around the letters, is sure to please both the gardening and nature lover

Designed by Helen Philipps

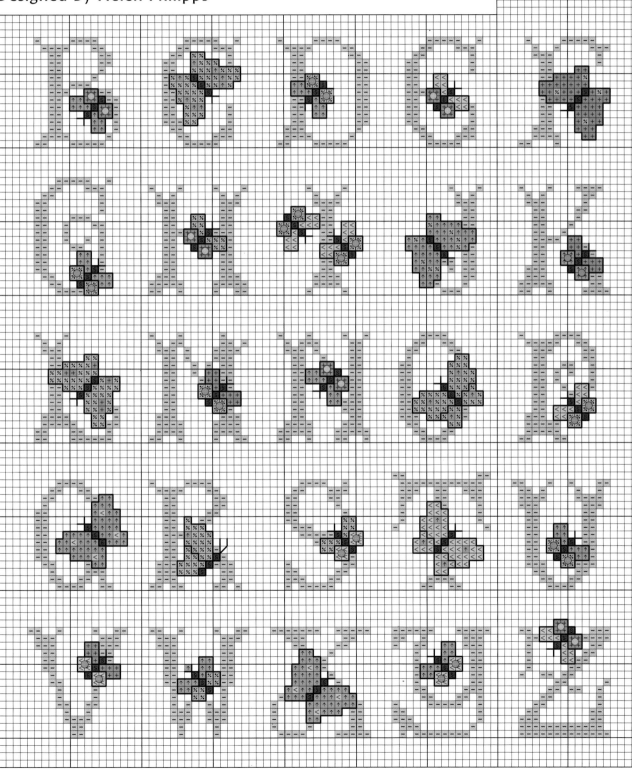

Xst

↑	340
−	554
<	726
%	742
S	839
+	976

BS

| ╱ | 317 |

FK

| | 742 |
| | 976 |

Teddies

Teddies rolling, tumbling and climbing; this fun alphabet is great for anyone who loves a friendly bear

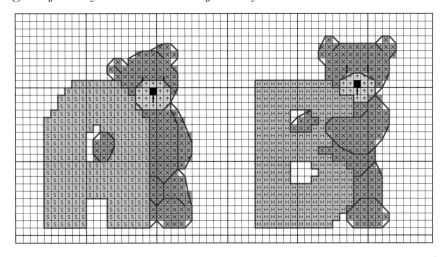

The towel band and bib were made from white 14 count aida fabric. The letters were stitched using DMC stranded cotton (floss), as listed in the key. Cut the towel band wide enough to fit across the towel, turn in the edges and stitch the band to the towel. Use a ready-made bib, or you can make your own by cutting the aida fabric into a circle, and then removing the top segment, before finishing the edge with cotton lace and neck ties.

Designed by Lesley Teare

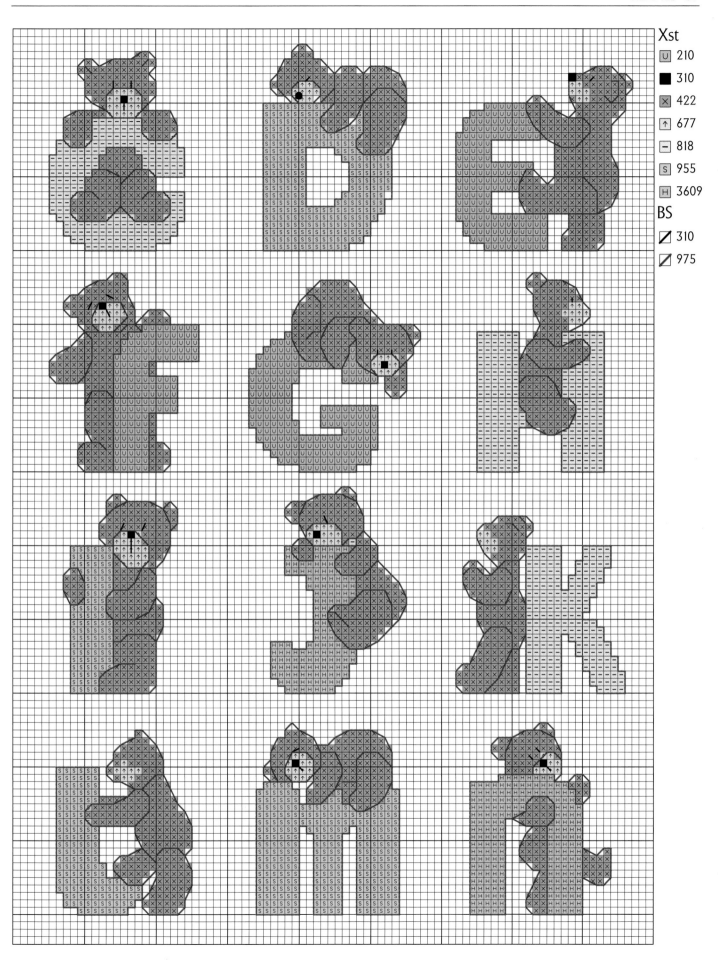

Xst

U	210
■	310
✕	422
↑	677
–	818
S	955
H	3609

BS

| ╱ | 310 |
| ╱ | 975 |

Xst

U	210
■	310
☒	422
↑	677
−	818
S	955
H	3609

BS

⁄	310
⁄	975

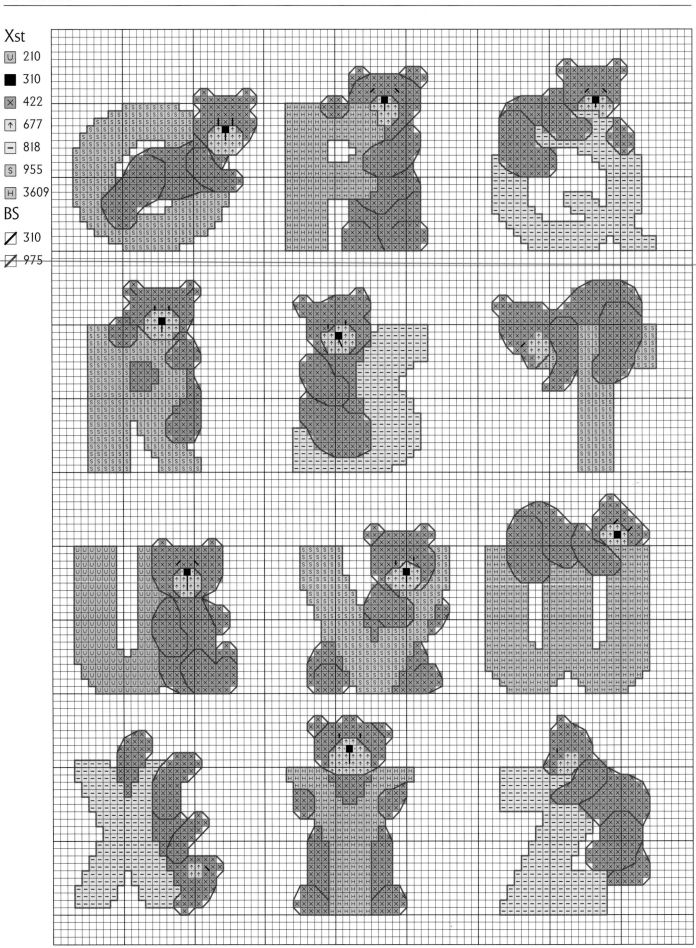

Sheep

Go down on to the farm with this cheerful alphabet featuring black-faced sheep, sleeping, jumping and having fun in the countryside

Designed by Caroline Palmer

Xst

- ⋅ Blanc
- ■ 310
- ▽ 347
- 4 415
- ∩ 552
- I 642
- ⁒ 726
- ◣ 741
- U 798
- H 911

BS

- ⁄ 310

Quilters

This delightful stitching set of needle case and pin cushion is a
wonderful gift for the quilting enthusiast

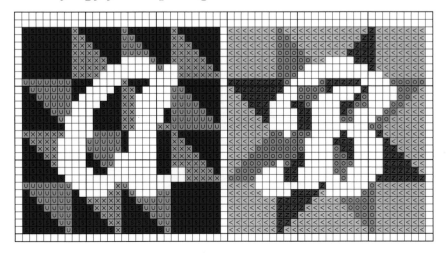

The pin cushion and needle case were worked on white 32 count antique white evenweave fabric using DMC stranded cotton (floss), as listed in the key. Each stitch should be worked over two threads of fabric. Once stitched, back the pin cushion with fabric and stuff before attaching cord to the edge. Leave extra fabric to the left of the design for the needle case. Line with fabric, and then stitch a felt flap inside to hold the needles. Fold in half and add cord ties.

Designed by Maria Diaz

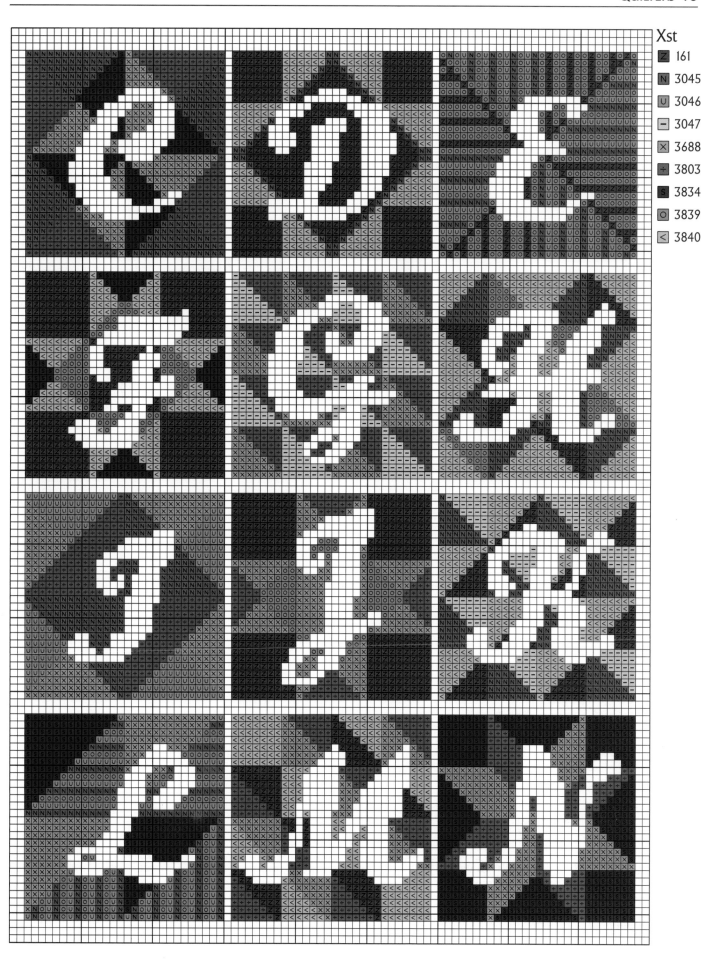

Xst

Z	161
N	3045
U	3046
−	3047
X	3688
+	3803
S	3834
O	3839
<	3840

Xst

Z	161
N	3045
U	3046
−	3047
X	3688
+	3803
S	3834
O	3839
<	3840

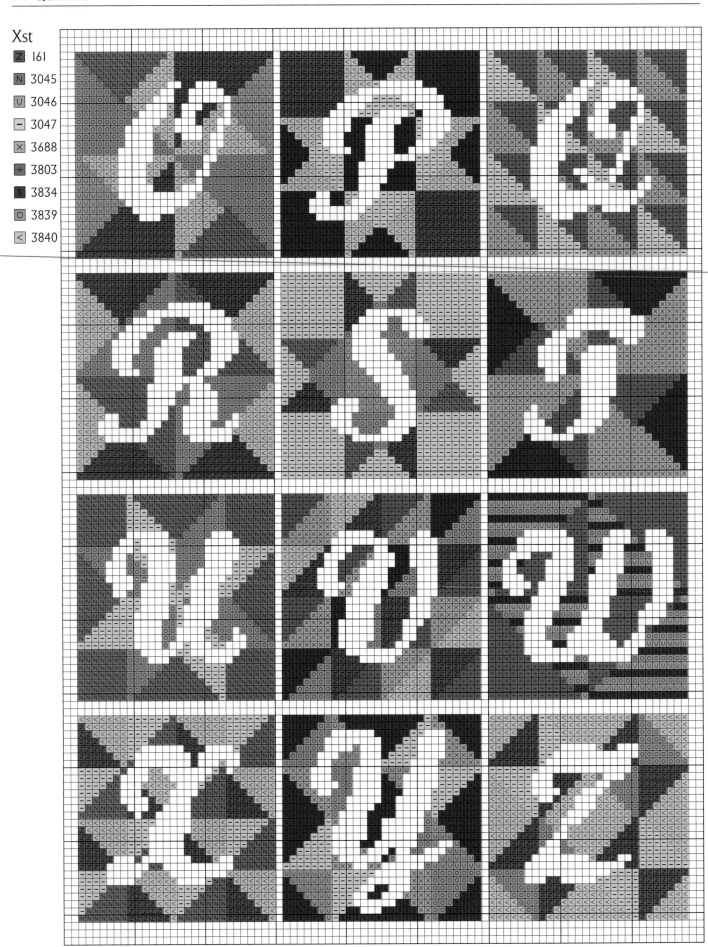

Stitchers

*Sewing enthusiasts will love this pretty alphabet which has many uses
from monogramming stitching equipment to making greetings cards*

Designed by Sue Cook

Xst

=	744
S	894
‖	3849

BS

⟋	317
⟋	3804

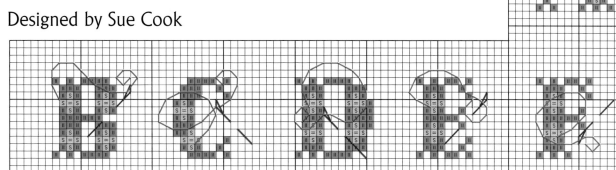

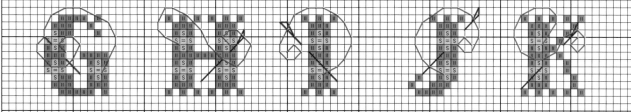

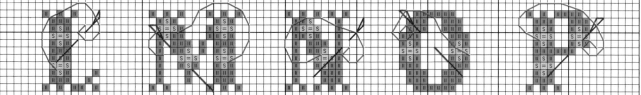

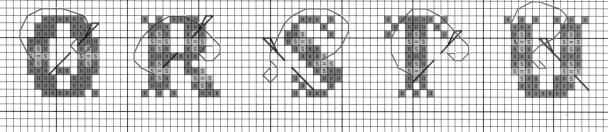

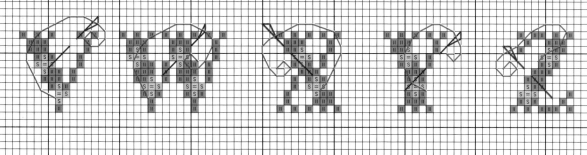

Nursery Rhymes

*Children love stories, so this delightful alphabet featuring some
of their favourite nursery rhymes is sure to become a favourite*

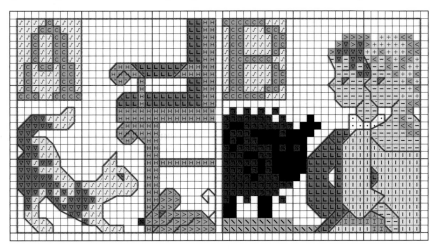

The card designs were worked on white 28
count evenweave fabric using DMC stranded
cotton (floss), in the colours listed in the
key, and working each stitch over two
threads of fabric.

Once mounted into cards the designs
were decorated with ribbon bows, buttons
and ribbon roses.

Letters from this alphabet could be
stitched together to make a nursery rhyme
frieze for a child's bedroom wall.

Designed by Claire Crompton

Xst
· Blanc
√ Ecru
U 209
↑ 210
■ 310
C 316
⌐ 333
N 407
◼ 413
= 415
< 422
▽ 435
> 437
T 505
◺ 562
◹ 563
⊥ 632
+ 677
– 754
◿ 777
S 791
∩ 792
▨ 898
I 3688
I 3689
F 3727
L 3831
Z 3835
O 3836
X 3839
→ 3840
H 3852

BS
╱ 898

FK
● 209
● 333
● 3831

Xst

- ⊡ Blanc
- ☑ Ecru
- Ⓤ 209
- ⬆ 210
- ■ 310
- Ⓒ 316
- ◪ 333
- Ⓝ 407
- ◪ 413
- ▤ 415
- ◁ 422
- ▽ 435
- ▷ 437
- ◪ 505
- ◰ 562
- ◩ 563
- ⊥ 632
- ⊞ 677
- − 754
- ◪ 777
- Ⓢ 791
- ⋒ 792
- ▨ 898
- ⊺ 3688
- Ⓘ 3689
- Ⓕ 3727
- Ⓛ 3831
- Ⓩ 3835
- Ⓞ 3836
- ⊠ 3839
- → 3840
- Ⓗ 3852

BS

- ◩ 898

FK

- ⬢ 209
- ⬤ 333
- ⬣ 3831

Clowns

These cheerful tumbling clowns are a fun way to brighten a plain nursery, or to send a birthday card to a special child

Designed by Claire Crompton

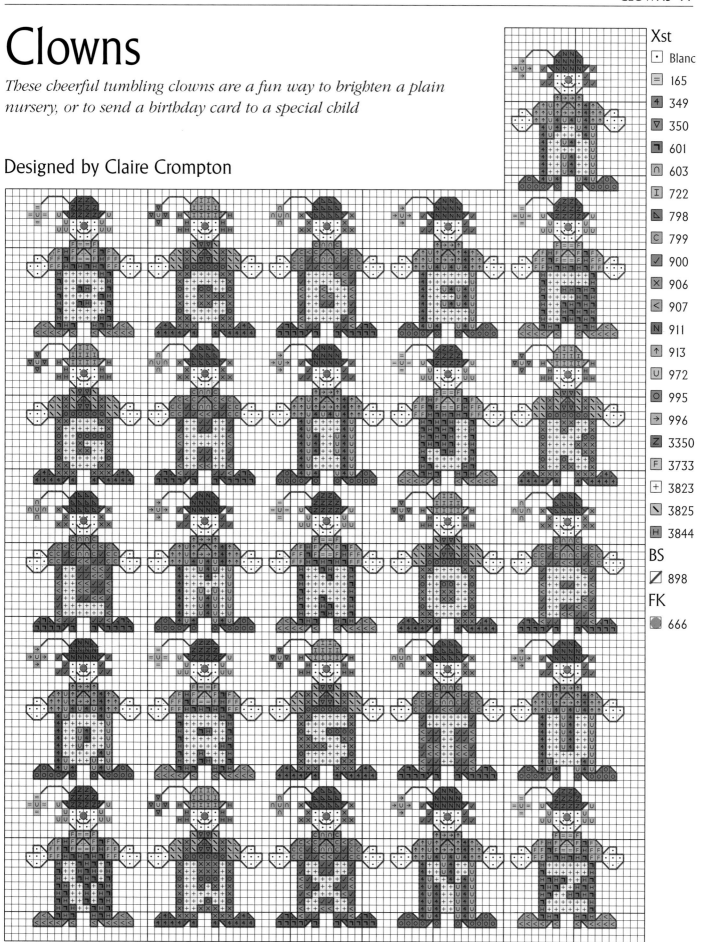

Xst	
·	Blanc
=	165
4	349
▽	350
⌐	601
∩	603
I	722
↳	798
C	799
✓	900
X	906
<	907
N	911
↑	913
U	972
O	995
→	996
Z	3350
F	3733
+	3823
◣	3825
H	3844

BS

╱	898

FK

| ⬡ | 666 |

Winter Woodland

*Rich brown dogwood is mixed with pink cyclamen and winter
jasmine to create a magical woodland alphabet*

The letters were stitched on platinum
14 count aida fabric using DMC stranded
cotton (floss), as listed in the key.

   After stitching each letter the fabric
pieces were cut to size, leaving the same
number of squares around each side of the
design. The edges were then frayed, before
attaching the designs to a handmade paper
bag and note book.

Designed by Susan Penny

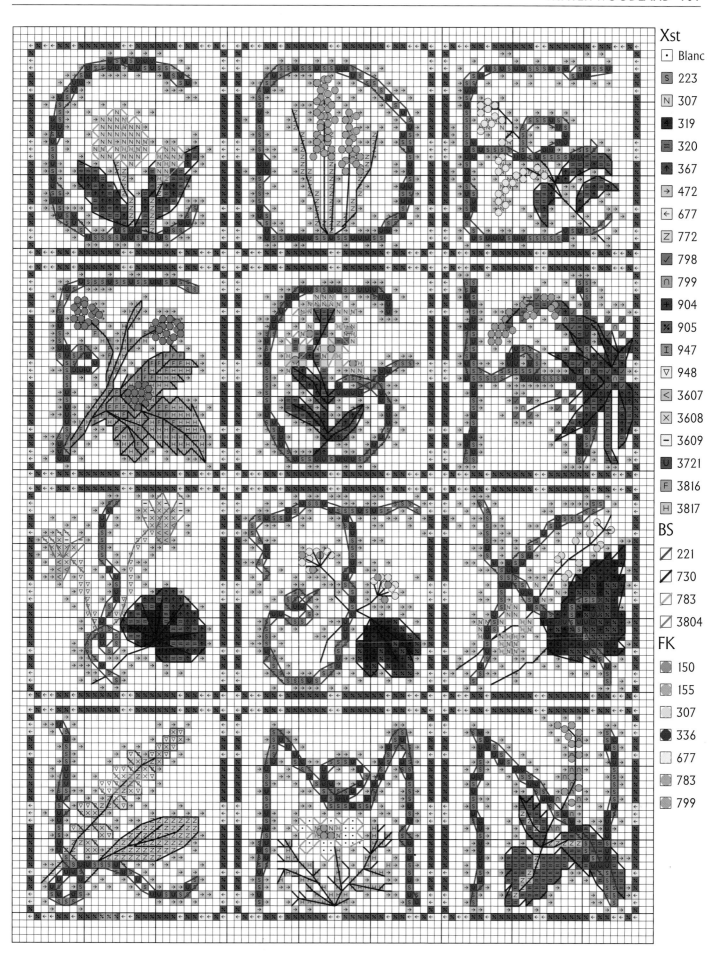

Xst

·	Blanc
S	223
N	307
✦	319
=	320
↑	367
→	472
←	677
Z	772
✓	798
∩	799
✚	904
✕	905
I	947
▽	948
<	3607
✕	3608
−	3609
U	3721
F	3816
H	3817

BS

╱	221
╱	730
╱	783
╱	3804

FK

●	150
●	155
●	307
●	336
●	677
●	783
●	799

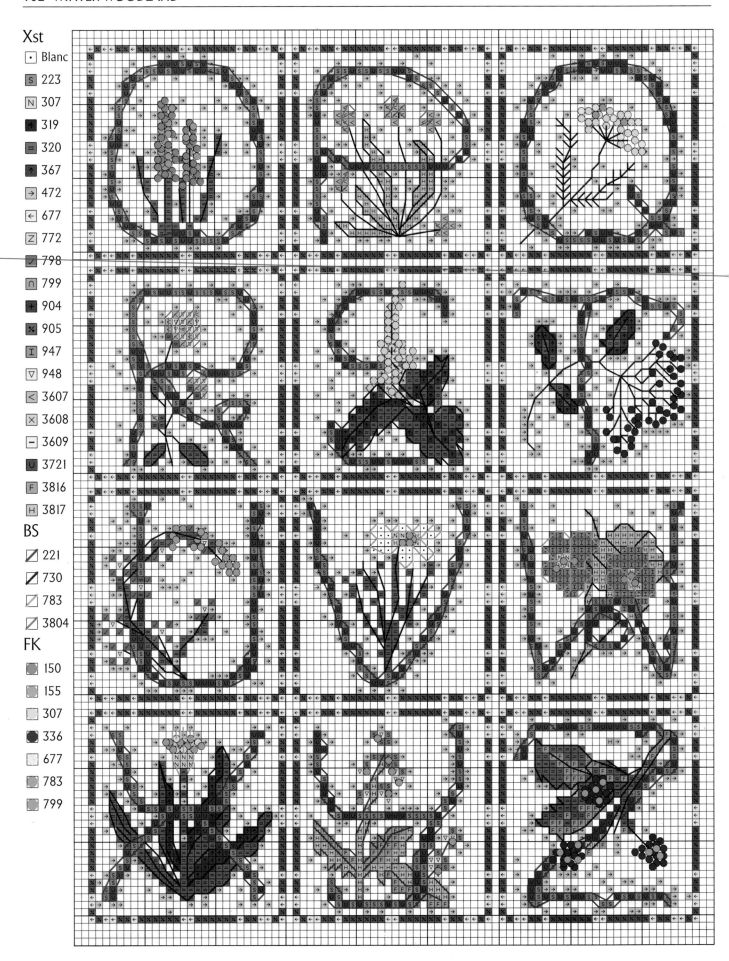

Summer Topiary

*This unusual alphabet, with each letter cut into the shape of a
topiary tree, is a great design for the gardening enthusiast*

Designed by Claire Crompton

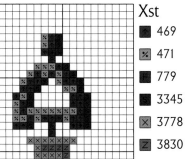

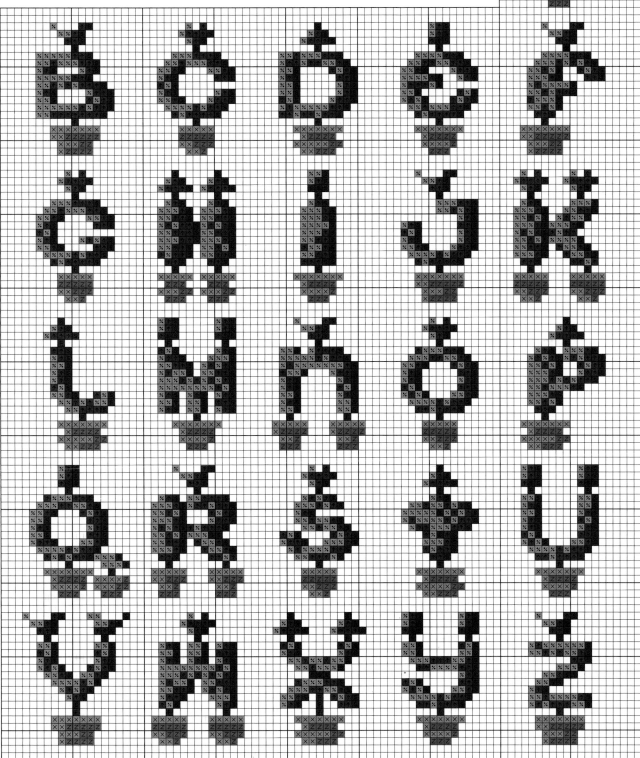

Stitching techniques

Most of the alphabets in this book are simple to stitch – a combination of cross stitch, backstitch and french knots. Below you will find working instructions for the stitches, and useful information on reading the charts

General stitching instructions

All the alphabets designs in this book use two strands of stranded cotton (floss) for the cross stitch and three-quarter stitches, and one strand for the backstitch and french knots.

Reading the charts

The charts are in colour, with a symbol printed in each square. Each square on the chart represents one cross stitch. In some cases, when working on finer fabric, each square on the chart is worked over two threads of fabric, if this is the case instructions will be given with the chart. All the charts have a key listing the DMC stranded cotton (floss) colours used in number order. The key also shows if there is backstitch, french knots or beads; the french knots and beads are shown as coloured dots on the key and chart. The beads are DMC and have been chosen to match the stranded cotton (floss) colours (more details on beads can be found in *Working with beads* on the next page). If you would prefer not to use beads then french knots can be used in their place.

Most designs have a combination of whole cross stitch, three-quarter stitch and backstitch. The three-quarter stitches are shown on the chart as triangles of colour printed in the corners of a square. As well as a chart and key, each design has a list of materials, instructions and a design size.

Understanding the charts

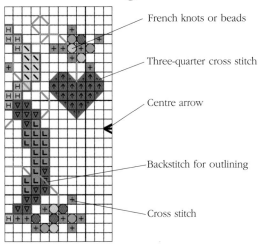

French knots or beads

Three-quarter cross stitch

Centre arrow

Backstitch for outlining

Cross stitch

A section of chart showing the stitches used on the designs in this book: cross stitch, three-quarter stitch, backstitch, french knots and beads.

Fabric

The designs in this book are worked on aida or evenweave fabric like linen. All the fabrics used for cross stitch should have the same number of horizontal and vertical threads to the inch. Aida has threads grouped together in blocks, so that one stitch is made over one block of threads using the holes as a guide. When working on the finer evenweave, like 36 count, the instructions may tell you to make each stitch over two or even four threads of fabric. A project sewn over two threads on 28 count fabric, for example, would come out the same size as if you stitched it on 14 count aida. The fabric listed in the key shows the count, the colour, and the actual size of fabric needed for the design. When buying the fabric allow extra at the edges if you are intending to work the design in a hoop or small frame. If you want to stitch on a different count of fabric than suggested in the project, you will have to calculate the finished size of the stitching before you buy the fabric. To do this, count the number of squares both high and wide of your chosen design – this is the stitch count. Then divide the two measurements by the number of threads per inch of your fabric. When you are stitching over two threads remember to divide the stitch count by half the number of threads per inch.

Needle and thread

Use a needle for cross stitch that is blunt and slips easily through the fabric without piercing it. A size 24 tapestry needle works best on 14 count aida, while a 26 tapestry needle is best for finer fabric. A 26 tapestry needle should easily pass through the eye of most beads, but you may find that using a fine sewing needle is easier on some designs. All the designs in this book are stitched with DMC stranded cotton. Unless specified in the instructions given with each design, two strands should be used for the cross stitch, and one for the backstitch and french knots. If DMC metallic thread has been included in the design, use two strands for the cross stitch, unless a different number of strands has been given in the instructions. On a few designs two different stranded cotton (floss) colours have been blended together in the needle, in most cases one strand of each colour should be used. Where Kreinek blending filament is used on a design, a single strand should be added to the needle with the stranded cotton (floss) colour.

Preparing to stitch

Cut your fabric several inches larger than the size given in the project materials list. Zig-zag around the edges of the fabric or bind it with masking tape to prevent the edges fraying. Fold the fabric in four to find the centre point, and mark it with a pin or small stitch. Find the centre of the chart by following the arrows from the edges to the centre – this is where you begin stitching. Thread your needle and make a knot at one end of the thread. Push the needle to the back of the fabric about 3cm (1¼in) from your starting point, leaving the knot on the right side. Stitch towards the knot, securing the thread on the back of the fabric. When the thread is secure, cut off the knot. Finish the thread by weaving it through the back of the stitches.

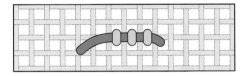

Hoop or frame

Most small designs can easily be stitched without mounting the fabric in a hoop or frame. If you do decide to use one, you will need to cut a larger piece of fabric than given in the materials list. Once the stitching has been completed the excess fabric can be cut away. Your project should always be removed from the hoop when you have finished stitching, to prevent a ring mark forming on the fabric.

Working with beads

The beads are shown on the charts and keys as coloured dots. For more details on understanding the charts and keys see *Reading the charts*, at the beginning of this chapter. All the beads used in this book match DMC stranded cotton (floss) colours. There are four different type of beads used: V1 general seed beads, V2 nostalgia, V3 metallic and V4 frosted. As well as the bead type, a colour code and colour description will also be listed. The beads should be attached to the stitching using two strands of stranded cotton (floss). Thread the bead on to the needle as you make the first part of the cross, then as you make the second part, lay one thread of stranded cotton (floss) either side of the bead, before pushing the needle back into the fabric and continuing.

Washing and pressing

Always wash your work before you mount it in a card or tag. To do this, swish the stitching in luke warm water and, if the colours bleed, rinse in fresh water until the water is clear. Do not be tempted to stop rinsing unless you are absolutely sure the bleeding has stopped. Roll the stitching in a clean towel and squeeze gently to remove most of the water. On a second towel, place your design face down, cover with a cloth and iron until dry.

Working the stitches

Cross stitch Each coloured square on the chart represents one cross stitch on the fabric. A cross stitch is worked in two stages: a diagonal stitch is worked over one block of aida, or two threads of finer evenweave fabric like linen, from the bottom left of the stitch to the top right. The second part of the stitch is worked from bottom right to top left to form a cross. When working a block of stitches in the same colour, stitch a line of half crosses before completing each stitch on the return journey. Make sure that the top half of each cross lies in the same direction.

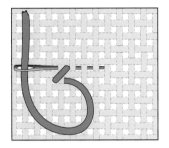

Three-quarter stitch Each stitch is shown on the chart as a coloured triangle. A three-quarter stitch is a half stitch (the first part of a cross stitch) with a quarter stitch worked from one of the remaining corners to the middle of the stitch. It is easier to work fractional stitches when each stitch is being worked over two threads of fabric (like linen or fine evenweave). When stitching on aida you will have to pierce the middle of the fabric block with a sharp needle to make a hole for the quarter stitch.

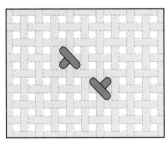

Backstitch This is shown on the chart as a solid coloured line, and may be used on the chart in several different ways: as an outline to give definition to an area of stitches; on top of the cross stitch to give detail; on its own, to create areas of lettering or detail lines. Backstitch can be worked as single stitches over one or two threads of fabric, or as longer stitches to cover a larger area.

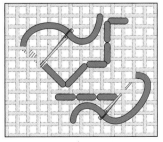

Acknowledgments

The publishers would like to thank the following people: Sue Cook, Claire Crompton, Maria Diaz, Lucie Heaton, Susan Penny, Caroline Palmer, Helen Philipps, Lesley Teare, Anne Wilson for their design contributions; Judy Davies, Angela Ottewell, Anne Swetman, Christine Thompson for their expert stitching; Doreen Holland for her chart checking; and Susan and Martin Penny for producing the book.

The following designers can be contacted at the addresses below:
Sue Cook at The August Moon Design Company Limited, 32 Wavell Drive, Malpas, Newport, Gwent NP20 6QN. Website: www.augustmoon.co.uk.
Susan Penny at Penny & Penny, 135 Bay View Road, Northam, Devon EX39 1BJ. email: penny.andpenny@virgin.net
Helen Philipps at Merry Heart Designs, PO Box 110, Hoylake, Wirral CH48 2WD. Website: www.merryheart.co.uk.

Suppliers

When writing to any of the companies below, please include a stamped addressed envelope for your reply.

DMC Creative World Ltd
Pullman Road, Wigston, Leicester LE8 2DY
Zweigart Aida, linen and stranded cotton.

Coats Crafts Ltd
PO Box 22, The Lingfield Estate, McMullen Road,
Darlington, Co Durham DL1 1YQ
Kreinek blending filament.

Craft Creations Ltd
2C Ingersoll House, Dalamare Road, Cheshunt, Herts
EN8 9ND
Card mounts.

Impress Cards & Craft Materials
Slough Farm, Westhall, Halesworth, Suffolk
IP19 8RN
Card mounts.

The DMC Corporation
Port Kearney Bld, 10 South Kearney,
NJ 070732-0650, USA
Zweigart Aida, linen and stranded cotton.

Gay Bowles Sales Inc
PO Box 1060, Janesville, WI, USA

Anne Brinkley Designs Inc
761 Palmer Avenue, Holmdel, NJ 97733, USA

Ireland Needlecraft Pty Ltd
2-4 Keppel Drive, Hallam, Victoria 3803, Australia

DMC Needlecraft Pty
PO Box 317, Earlswood 2206, New South Wales
2204, Australia
Zweigart Aida, linen and stranded cotton.

Conversion Chart

DMC	Anchor	DMC	Anchor	DMC	Anchor	DMC	Anchor	DMC	Anchor
151		452	232	743	305	955	*206	3765	169
155		453	231	745	300	956	38	3772	1007
157		469	*267	747	158	957	*50	3777	1015
161		471	*255	754	1012	959	185	3778	1013
163		501	877	758	*882	963	968	3779	4146
164		502	876	762	234	967		3799	236
165		503	875	772	*1043	972	*298	3803	69
167		505		777		973	290	3805	*62
168		543	933	778	1016	975	370	3810	*168
169		553	*99	779		977	1002	3811	928
208	*111	562	*208	780	365	989	*261	3813	*1042
209	*109	563	*204	783	307	993	186	3814	189
210	108	597	168	791	213	995	410	3820	306
211	34	601	*63	792	177	996	433	3822	*305
221	1015	602	63	792	177	3011	924	3823	386
301	349	603	62	793	176	3012	*855	3825	1047
309	39	604	*55	797	147	3013	*854	3829	*907
310	black	605	60	798	137	3045	888	3830	5975
312	*148	610	889	799	145	3046	887	3831	29
316	971	611	898	807	168	3047	*886	3834	100
317	*400	612	*888	817	46	3051	*268	3835	98
318	399	613	853	818	*271	3064	*883	3836	90
321	47	632	371	823	152	3078	292	3837	100
327	101	642	392	838	381	3325	*144	3838	177
333	*606	644	830	822	926	3341	*328	3839	176
340	118	666	9046	890	1044	3345	263	3840	117
349	13	676	891	898	360	3347	266	3841	159
350	*11	677	886	900	*332	3348	254	3844	*410
351	10	701	*227	906	256	3350	69	3846	*1090
352	9	702	226	907	*255	3362	263	3852	306
369	1043	704	256	910	229	3363	262	3858	*1007
402	1047	720	*326	911	*230	3364	*260	3859	*914
407	914	721	*324	913	*204	3371	382		
413	236	722	*323	924	851	3607	87	3865	2
414	*400	725	305	926	850	3608	86	3866	926
415	398	726	297	928	274	3609	85	Blanc	White
420	*277	727	293	928	274	3687	68	Ecru	926
422	373	728		930	922	3688	*1016		
434	310	729	890	931	1034	3689	49	* Not an exact match	
435	1046	738	942	932	343	3727	1016		
436	1045	739	1009	948	1011	3733	*66		
437	362	742	303	950	376	3753	1031